WHAT WAS GOOD ABOUT TODAY

What Was Good About Today

CAROL
KRUCKEBERG

A DELL BOOK

Published by
Dell Publishing Co., Inc.
1 Dag Hammarskjold Plaza
New York, New York 10017

Dell ® TM 681510, Dell Publishing Co., Inc.

ISBN: 0-440-19425-3

Reprinted by arrangement with Madrona Publishers, Inc.
Printed in the United States of America

March 1986

10 9 8 7 6 5 4 3 2 1

WFH

For those who danced for Sara

Janet Thomas
January 1987

What Was Good About Today

Sara

ONE

THE tissue-paper sheeting crackles as Sara squirms impatiently on the examining table. She picks at the Band-Aid on her arm from where the blood was drawn, then swallows a little belch, the result of two bottles of pop swigged down in the last thirty minutes. In mock indignation I flare my nostrils and Walt furrows his brow. But our feigned disgust melts into laughter when Sara hunches her shoulders and grins her guilty grin. It has been five days since we've glimpsed those dimples, and relief shivers through us. She seems better and we are embarrassed to be in this emergency room listening to the screams of a child with broken bones, the labored gasps of a heart-attack victim and the raunchy ravings of a drunk. This place is for sick people, not a kid with the flu. If only they would hurry with the results of her blood tests we could bundle her back into the quilted rosebud robe and go home, assured she is recovering.

Time blurs by, the big clock hums, voices murmur outside our room and there are furtive glances our way as strangers huddle over a sheet of yellow paper. An empty space is born inside me and my hands are sticky cold. Walt's car keys chink from one hand to the other.

"Sara, would you like another pop while I go for a walk with your mom and dad?" asks Dr. Wendy. "We need to discuss a little problem." Sara smiles an OK. I kiss her soft plump cheek, noticing it is still fevered, and promise to come right back. She twirls her brown eyes heavenward. I am forever a mother hen. Wendy stalks ahead with mustered efficiency and Walt is dragging me, for my legs are inoperable. We tumble down the rabbit's hole into a glaring fluorescence, the Nurses' Lounge. The chair is cold, the table is cold and my empty space has grown and frozen over. I shudder uncontrollably. My hands and Walt's hands are heaped together on the tabletop and when I look at Walt he is an old man. Dr. Wendy's hands pile on ours and she says, "There is something very wrong with Sara's blood . . ."

"Yes," I interrupt. "She has leukemia." Spoken as if it were a guilty secret I had borne eternally.

Walt says, "Shut up" (Oh Walt, we don't allow those words in our home!), but Wendy confirms this is a real possibility. Our journey begins.

Even as we stumble back to Sara, Walt and I whisper strategy. Without our being aware of it, our roles are set in concrete tonight.

Sara has been whisked into the world of white. Dr. Wendy bristles to find her with a roommate when isolation was ordered. We shrivel upon learning that Sara has no immunities. And we tag along, hangdog, as our doctor personally maneuvers Sara's bed to its private cubicle.

While strangers take over the care of our daughter, Walt

and I huddle in the maternity waiting room near where Sara was born. And we act. It is Walt who will go home and tend to the life that goes on. It is Walt who will tell my mom and dad the horrible suspicion. It is Walt who will explain to five-year-old Andy, staying the night with Grandma and Grandpa, why Mama and Sissy must leave without kissing him goodbye. And Walt will sleep alone for the first time since Andy's birth. We cling together affirming and reaffirming our ability to cope. We are not all that convincing.

Dr. Wendy slips in to brief us on our itinerary. At seven the next morning, Sara will be transported by ambulance to Children's Orthopedic Hospital in Seattle, where tests can be performed to confirm the suspected diagnosis. I will ride with her and Walt will follow in our car. I nod as if I understand, but I am thinking that this journey was booked without our knowledge or consent. And where do they get off stealing our self-control? And just who are "they" anyway? Walt kisses our tangle-haired sleepy girl goodnight, stretching awkwardly over the IV tubing as it pumps antibiotics into Sara's veins. In the hall we touch goodbye. "Try and sleep," we say. A sick joke. The elevator door severs our communication. I sag back. And all alone support the wall.

It is time to deal with Sara. Already she has endured chest X rays, cultures drawn from every body orifice, IV needles and an extensive physical examination. The procedures are administered with excruciating care, unnatural gentleness and dreaded foreknowledge. There is a serenity about Sara as she sizes up my puffed eyes and forced smile. The questions are there and she waits until I am ready to talk turkey.

The lone window in our cell is small and high, offering no possibility of a getaway. Silently we watch the smoke from the mill bilge grey into the night sky and dissipate over the harbor.

"Pollution disgusts me," Sara offers. I accept her clue and know that the information Sara receives from me must be clear and honest. She is passive yet pleased at the prospect of the ambulance ride and accepts without comment that tomorrow we will find out for sure what is causing her sore throat and temperature.

While I pet her slender "piano-hands," she finally sleeps. Her hair, blonde-streaked, fever-damp, spills curly all over the pillow. Her bones are long, like Walt's bones. When she plays soccer she is a wild pony, mane tossing in the wind. She runs faster than any boy on her team but is more apt to throw a cartwheel on the field than to kick the ball. She calls her uniform a costume and wears ribbons to match her shorts on game days. When she tells her dad to hurry so they won't be late for rehearsal on practice afternoons, he knows she is no jock.

The alarm on Sara's IV pump buzzes, signaling the end of my game. The nurse rustles in to tend the machine. "Can I get you a Valium?" she asks in a stage whisper. "Doctor ordered one up for you."

"I do not take drugs," I mutter primly. Sara sleeps soundly so I melt away to escape the nurse's curious glance.

Wandering the empty hall, I decide I am too young for this. I need to talk to Mom and Dad. The eleven o'clock news blares from somebody's room. As I dial, I half listen for a coast-to-coast flash reporting Sara's illness. I say, "Hi, Daddy," and he cries and I cry and the nurse at the phone desk cries. It occurs to me that they, also, are too young for this. We talk about Andy, and Mama says that he is a tough guy. I feel good knowing they will be there to fill the gaps for him. I feel sad realizing that because of me their pain is doubled.

I drift back to Sara. Dr. Wendy is watching her sleep. With our elbows locked together like schoolgirls, we trudge to the waiting room. The vinyl squeaks obscenely when we collapse on the couch, holding hands. We met four hours ago and now we are best friends. I look Wendy in the eye and I quietly begin my defense.

First off, the pregnancy was planned. I took vitamins, drank lots of milk, ate a well-balanced diet, gained eighteen pounds, and indulged in a glass of wine only on special occasions. I breast-fed and buckled Sara into a government-approved car seat even to ride around the block. We buggied daily for fresh air and she never ate presweetened cereal or any that contained BHA or BHT additives. Sara grew tall. She grew bright and beautiful. She grew happy. She was a gift of God. Indeed, her very birth was my affirmation that God existed. Therefore, I reason, we did it all right. Sara cannot logically have cancer. The defense rests.

My jury leans in to listen, nods sympathetically, and speaks slowly, reminding me that the final verdict is not in. Certain viruses imitate leukemia, and only the bone-marrow aspiration performed by the higher court in Seattle can be proof positive, one way or the other.

There is my straw to grasp! A virus. I relax as Wendy tells of her recent internship at Children's Orthopedic, of the strong and of the weak. Of the ability to live one day at a time.

When I return to my wheelchair bed in Sara's room it is three in the morning. I am armed with a full slate of events for today, Monday, May 5, plus the name of the presiding judge in Seattle, the hematology fellow on call, Dr. Dan Baker.

We journey to Seattle in a thick fog, though the ambulance driver complains of the glaring spring sunshine. We are the last vehicle inched onto the ferry, and when we tug away from the slip I wave to Walt who must wait thirty minutes for the next ferry. He slumps against the hood of our car.

In the ferryboat rest room, Bernice, a friend from Sequim, says, "How are you?"

I answer, "Fine." Then, horrified by my reply, I yank on the linen towel roll and tearfully blurt that I am not fine, Sara is in an ambulance and Walt is left behind on the dock. In the arms of Bernice, I spill the details of our last twelve hours.

Suspended animation reigns in that rest room. After a short stunned silence, motion returns; toilets flush, faucets splash, feet shuffle. Nameless faceless friends pat my sorrowing shoulders as they exit. I return to Sara and we glide into Seattle on the power generated by Bernice and the silent strangers.

Down the rabbits hole!

TWO

D<small>R</small>. Dan Baker's shaggy head dips to clear the doorway. Brown-bearded, wrinkled and untucked, he is the same age as my younger brother. He talks too fast, I listen too slow. His eyes, behind wire-rimmed glasses, are intense. Mine, behind gravel-lined lids, are unfocused. He is hyper. I am exhausted.

Dr. Baker delays further questioning to prepare for the bone-marrow aspiration. He is perpetual forward motion, head and shoulders in the lead, long legs following. He attacks the hallway, leaving us breathless and bemused. Maybe we will like him.

While Walt and I unpack, Sara and her nurse tend to the business of becoming best friends. Sara is incredulous over her plastic basin full of hospital goodies. She exclaims over each item as if she is plucking toys from a Christmas stocking. Nurse Nancy says she uses Baby Magic Lotion to keep her newly engaged hands soft, so Sara flips the lid from her sample bottle and offers Nancy a squeeze. Rubbing their hands together, they bond. And I know Nancy will belong to Sara's good times.

While Nancy brushes Sara's hair, teaching her to "feather" her bangs, Dr. Baker returns to explain the bone-marrow procedure. A long hollow needle will be inserted into Sara's hipbone, and marrow will be drawn quickly into a syringe. The bad news is that it will hurt. The good news is that it is over quickly and a choice from the Red Box, a treasure chest of toys, awaits as the reward. Dr. Baker asks Sara if she has any questions before we wheel into the treatment room.

"Do you know I have a dog and two cats?" she mumbles.

"I mean about the bone-marrow aspiration, Sara."

She bites her lip and continues brushing her hair.

The explanation of the bone-marrow aspiration puts us on edge, but its actuality shoves us over.

Sara lies on her belly with a pillow bunched under her hips. When her pink flowered panties are gently pulled down, she whimpers, embarrassed. I sit on a rolling three-legged stool, holding Sara's hot hand. Walt stands on the other side of the table stroking her thick natural curls. When my eyes meet Walt's eyes there is startled recognition. Without a word, a touch, a sign, we are one-minded. We ache to lie down on this table for Sara. We ache to lay down our lives for Sara. These are not options, so we do all we can. We stand by her.

Dr. Baker carefully explains each move. "There will be no surprises, Sara. First we wash the area three times. It will feel cold. Here goes number one." A sterile tweezer clamps a soaked gauze pad and swabs Sara's hip. She flinches and sniffles quietly.

"Number two." She shivers and her bleary brown eyes pinch shut.

"Last time, Sara. Number three." She squeezes my hand

hard and our tears splotch the sheet.

"Now, a little shot like you get at the dentist. It will numb your skin. You know, just a little pinprick."

"She has never had Novocain," I hastily explain, "because she has never even had a cavity."

While we wait for the anesthetic to take effect, Dr. Baker leans against the supply drawers, holding his sterile gloved hands in front of him. He chats with Sara about her dog and two cats, but she is too busy making goose bumps to answer.

The nurse, the intern and the lab technician draw in close and Dr. Baker says, "You will feel pressure, Sara, because I am pushing on your back." His probing latexed fingers hit the mark.

"You must hold absolutely still, Sara. Here we go." The needle plunges in and Dr. Baker's big body bears down on it. Sara moans as it penetrates bone.

"I am going to draw the marrow, Sara. This will hurt." Her moaning increases. She is wild-eyed, cornered. A piercing wail is cut short. Pain has taken her breath away.

And then it is over. The syringe is full of red fluid, distinguished from blood only by its bright color. The lab technician hustles it out the door, Sara is bandaged, and we beat a hasty retreat to lick our wounds.

While Walt and I still reel from the horror of our little girl's pain, Sara breaks the silence with a snort. "The toys in that Red Box better be good. That's all I've got to say!"

Sara studies, ponders, then plucks from the box a tiny kissing doll boasting self-inking lips. Tiny lip prints bloom in Sara's room. While she decorates, Walt and I stare out the window awaiting the verdict.

What a view from our third-floor window. Just last month our family visited that Space Needle. During spring vacation we splurged through Seattle; a hotel, the aquarium, the zoo, *The Lady and the Tramp*, a bib-and-tuckered restaurant, allowances jangling in red plastic squeeze purses, and then the finale. Dressed in pioneer garb, we posed prim and grim for a brown-toned family portrait at the Sundance Studios. While Walt, Andy and I nervously tittered, then scambled into our dress-up clothes, Sara solemnly chose a burgundy satin gown with ecru lace cape, a matching sunbonnet and a plastic bouquet. We smirked at her distant expression, acknowledging that, once again, Sara was gone, and in her place stood turn-of-the-century Laura Ingalls Wilder, heroine of Sara's favorite series, the Little House books.

She stashed those stories strategically: under her bed, behind the toilet, in couch cushions, on the back seat of the car and at Grandma's house. Occasionally Walt and I became Ma and Pa, Andy answered to Almanzo, the love of Laura's life, and our black lab, Muffin, shrugged her simple shoulders and loped along with the Great Pretender, who called her Jack.

None of us minded. After all, Laura provided welcome relief from the months of Dorothy and *The Wizard of Oz*. Walt had difficulty getting into the role of the Cowardly Lion. My self-image suffered as the Wicked Witch of the West. Andy found the Tin Woodsman boring, and Muffin was a ridiculous Toto.

In red high heels, Sara storked around the neighborhood with pantyhose pulled onto her head, their legs dangling, blue ribbons tied at the ends. She wore them day and night. She answered curious stares with, "Dorothy's braids, don't you know." During those days we swallowed hard and looked the other way. During those nights we stealthily removed the pantyhose, fearing cranial jock itch.

We endured and enjoyed not only Laura and Dorothy. Janet Lynn, Olympic figure skater, leaped our living room; Nadia Comaniche, Romanian gymnast, flip-flopped our family room; Cleopatra, Queen of the Nile, draped the red wagon; Pinky Tuscadero, "Happy Days" motorcyclist, wheelied our driveway; and Lolly, little lost Alaskan on the "Wonderful World of Disney," nearly got us arrested at Nordstrom's Department Store.

Pigtails drooped and saddle shoes dangled as Sara sat slouched in Nordstrom's shoe department. It was the end of a long day of big-city shopping. As I browsed I kept a watchful eye on my four-year-old daughter, the chubby-cheeked cherub in the red velvet fur-trimmed coat. Then, without warning, a mournful wail echoed around the shoe boxes.

"Mommy! I want my mommy!"

"I'm right here, darling."

"I mean my *real* mommy. Take me home."

"Sara, sweetheart . . ."

"Please don't call me Sara. You know my name is Lolly."

"Sara Beth, that will do!"

"Lolly wants to go home to her real mommy."

Strangers squinted suspiciously at my blotchy neck as we firmly exited stage right. Halfway through the revolving door, Lolly turned to her audience. She bowed. And she blew a kiss.

But now it is not Laura, Dorothy, Janet, Cleopatra, Pinky or Lolly lying nearby. It is Sara. And this is for real.

Dr. Baker returns and wants assurance that Sara understands that he did not want to hurt her during the bone-marrow aspiration. It was the only way to determine the cause of her illness. Will she forgive him? She eyeballs him judiciously, then grins and inks a tiny kiss on his forearm. He touches her cheek, but does not return her smile. He says, "Keep on truckin', Sara. We'll be right back." And for the second time in as many days, we wearily trail a young stranger.

The conference room opens off the third-floor television lounge. A small group of cleaning ladies cluster around the TV, honed in on an afternoon soap. Dr. Baker closes the door, paces across the floor and folds into a chair. He hugs himself, arms crisscrossed, and he says that Sara's marrow is leukemic. Walt covers his face with his hands. I close my eyes and cover my ears, but I still see and I still hear. Dr. Baker lectures on leukemia.

There are two kinds of acute leukemia. Acute lymphocytic leukemia, A.L.L., is the most common and most responsive to treatment. Acute myeloblastic leukemia, A.M.L., is rare and difficult to treat. For positive diagnosis, Sara's marrow has been sent to the University of Washington laboratory. However, it is the consensus of the physicians who studied the sample that Sara's leukemia is probably lymphocytic. Dr. Baker says we are lucky, A.L.L. is the "good" kind, usually treated successfully. Over ninety percent of A.L.L. children achieve remission within weeks, and many never relapse. We nod vacantly at our "luck," and Dr. Baker leaves us alone.

We are close, quiet and rational. The diagnosis is no surprise. Like a pair of Pollyannas, we count our blessings. Our hospital is warm and comfortable, its people gentle and caring. Sara likes it here. And most important, we are winners. We sing, dance and laugh our lives away. Not even cancer whips a winner.

When Dr. Baker returns, we have our act together and we're ready to hit the hall. All three of us will talk to Sara about her disease and course of treatment. I tell Dr. Baker that Sara is familiar with leukemia. A friend at church has it, and she is involved in the community concern for him. Shoulders back, heads high, three abreast and invincible, we return to Sara.

Dr. Baker begins, "Sara, we have determined that you have a blood disease called leukemia. Do you know anything about it?"

A calculating silence, eyes roaming the floor, fingers picking the bedspread, and then, softly, "Never heard of it."

Dr. Baker looks startled, "Your mom told me you know a child with leukemia, Sara. Is that true?"

"Beats me."

With a soft smile, laced with perspiration and exasperation, Dr. Baker edges onto Sara's bed. He explains that her infection-fighting white cells are multiplying too rapidly. They are not maturing into adult cells capable of getting rid of her sore throat and fever. She needs strong medicine to deal with these leukemia cells. Does she understand?

Sara continues lint-picking, then suddenly flashes her tremendous grin, announces she feels great and is ready to draw. Please pass the Magic Markers.

Dr. Baker is bothered and bewildered, but I am bewitched.

How quickly she has set about the task at hand, and in such a predictable way. How does any artist deal with adversity? With a rush of pride and exhilaration, I hand over her medium.

While Sara draws, Dr. Baker suggests Walt and I find something to eat. He directs us to the cafeteria. We weave through a maze of colorful muraled halls, stand dazed in the sluggish elevator, bump onto the fifth floor to find the cafeteria locked. Dinner is over.

A custodian sends us winding back to the first-floor snack machines. Confused and disoriented in this sprawling building, I clutch Walt and tell him not to lose me. I could never find my way back. He snaps, "You can do what you have to do."

In the smoky haze of the brilliantly lit snack bar, stress strikes our appetites, enraging Walt's and killing mine. I gag on half a cheese sandwich while Walt chunks change into the machines as if expecting to hit the jackpot. Finally filled, he announces it is time to head back, and things feel better now.

Sara sleeps soundly, so we drag our phone into the hall and begin informing relatives and friends of the diagnosis. We chant a hundred times, "We are lucky. It's the good kind. We will beat it."

By midnight we can no longer walk, talk or think. There is a blue plastic couch in Sara's room that folds out into a little bed. Walt and I tuck in, needing to be close, like spoons. It is a good thing. In this bed there is no other option.

The IV pump sputters intermittently, the clock buzzes hourly, Sara groans, feverish, and the night drags on.

We've been informed that Sara's vital signs will be checked every few hours. But, still, I startle at 4:00 a.m. to find a wild-eyed man telling jokes to Sara.

"What's green and runs backward?"

"I don't know."

He answers with a wet exaggerated snort.

Sara pauses, puzzled; then brightens, gasps, and finally laughs out loud. "Oh, gross!"

I bolt upright and the man whispers, "Don't mind me. I'm Adrian, the loose guy on the floor tonight." I determine to stand guard against this hospital jester with the marginal sense of humor. I pull on my jeans and wander the hallway, aware for the first time that we share B-3 with seven other cancer families. Today I want to know them, pick their brains, and be reassured that we too can deal.

Tuesday, May 6, 7:00 a.m. The shift changes on B-3. Adrian, jacketed and bent beneath a blue backpack, is headed home to sleep away this grey day. But not before he offers a sincere apology, a formal introduction and a cup of coffee.

He is sorry he startled me in the night. He is an aide on B-3 and usually works evenings, three to eleven. He shoves the steamy black peace offering my way and says Sara is super. I grudge up a grin and decide to give the guy another chance.

Morning marches on. Nurses bustle with breakfasts, baths and bed changes. Lab technicians balance trays for blood draws. Parents shuffle to the shower. Eight televisions tune to the "New Zoo Revue."

Nurse Nancy, Sara, the IV pump and I parade to the tub room where Sara bathes and shampoos. We dawdle the morning away primping, powdering and pretending.

Cleaning ladies, Blue Ladies, aides, nurses and interns pause to pet Sara's hair, her beribboned sausage curls. She is the only patient on B-3 with hair.

While Sara dozes and dreams away the wet afternoon, Walt observes that her room is beginning to look like her room at home. Sara the Artist has strewn creations everywhere. Sara the Saver has stockpiled uneaten tidbits in preparation for the next Great Depression. And Sara the Vamp has perfumed every portion of her beautiful body.

"It smells like a French whorehouse in here," Walt whispers. Dr. Baker intrudes on our laughter with his hurried-worried entrance. He quickly introduces us to the social worker in tow, and says the results of Sara's bone-marrow stains are back from the University and we need to discuss them.

He leads, we follow, and the social worker snags a box of Kleenex and brings up the rear.

Same conference room, same seating assignments, same uncontrollable quivering, same teeth-chattering frozen grip. But now a scent of something too horrible to hear, too heavy to bear.

"I'm so sorry. The stains conclude that Sara has acute myeloblastic leukemia."

They calmly watch us fall apart as if we are subjects of a scientific study. They look aghast at what they see.

Disbelief. Horror. Terror. Desperation. Anger. Hatred.

Like a cornered animal, I lash at Dr. Baker. I sneer and mimic yesterday's pompous rhetoric, "We believe in dealing honestly with parents and patients. They cope better that way." Ha! We coped with yesterday's diagnosis, but now he has changed the game. And there are new rules in this game.

Walt wants to hear them, but Dr. Baker says we need a little time to digest the new information before we discuss it further. He backs out the door. The social worker reaches toward me, but I grab at her Kleenex and flinch away. She follows Dr. Baker.

Alone. I scrunch on the floor in the corner. Walt slams on the wall with his fists. Over and over again. The noises we make are not human.

Then finally our ears hear, our eyes focus and our bodies touch. The world turns once again. We hunker together on the couch with nothing to say. Dr. Baker returns.

Now he instructs us on the rules of this new game. Fifty percent of A.M.L. children have an initial remission. Fifty percent do not.

Of those children who attain a first remission, ninety-five percent relapse within a year. A lasting second remission is unknown.

Dr. Baker apologizes for the failures of himself, modern medicine and cancer research. Walt interrupts and asks the unthinkable.

"Are you saying that there is a ninety-five percent chance that Sara will be dying within the year?"

Dr. Baker shrugs and nods.

Walt says, "Damn it. We've never even been to Disneyland."

While Walt urgently plans a trip to the Magic Kingdom, Dr. Baker carefully traces the wale of his corduroys and I desperately plan a new attack.

Where fear and anger failed to gain Sara a reprieve, logic will prevail. This unjust god must see the error of his ways.

Listen up, Dr. Baker. "Her teachers say she is compassionate, sensitive to the needs of others, gentle and caring. She excels academically. She attends a special class for gifted artists."

Listen up, Dr. Baker. "When we visit the nursing home, Sara takes charge. She caresses white hair, lotions dry skin, and brushes false teeth. She recites poetry, sings camp songs, and 'remembers when' with old ladies. When I get restless I whisper, 'Get the lead out of your fanny, Granny. Time to go home!' She frowns and lingers a little longer."

Listen up, Dr. Baker. "Sara has a brother to raise. She fixes his cereal on Saturday morning, drags out his kitty blanket when he is cold, takes his part in neighborhood squabbles. She is her brother's keeper."

Dr. Baker keeps nodding, nodding, nodding. Mumbling, "Yes, yes, yes. I recognized her specialness and it will help her cope."

"You did not listen to me," I spit. "She should not have to cope. She is compassionate, sensitive, gentle, caring, kind, gifted, nice to old ladies and little brothers. She is mine and you cannot sentence her to die."

Dr. Baker smudges at his steamy glasses with hospital Kleenex and says he must talk to us about protocol, the course of treatment for Sara's cancer. I look him in the eye to let him know that though we've lost this battle we haven't lost the war.

The protocol for A.M.L. is experimental. We will sign a release acknowledging that there are dangerous side effects and no guarantees. Sara will receive two chemicals intravenously: Ara-C will drip for seven days and Adriamycin will be injected in three pushes. She will be given a seven-day rest and then a second course of chemotherapy.

Dr. Baker says, "If remission is attained, we look toward maintenance; more chemotherapy and radiation to the head."

"You will not mess with Sara's head," I snarl. "No radiation."

While I fight hysteria, Dr. Baker explains that the dosage will not affect Sara's brain. Cranial radiation is given prophylactically, because without it, A.M.L. may reappear in the central nervous system. In fact, today he will perform a spinal tap to see if leukemic cells are already present.

Dr. Baker sees we are on the edge of insanity and says it is enough for today. He releases the thumbscrews, tucks the consent forms under Walt's arm, and points us back to B-3.

In the early evening gloom of that hallway we stand and bawl. Cattle with no calves. The rest of B-3's stricken herd gathers near. Their breath warms us. They stand ready to catch us if we fall.

Sara calls, "Mama!" I snap like a yo-yo at the end of its string and begin my ascent. When I reach Sara she grabs me and I am on top again.

She needs to use the bathroom and is embarrassed to ask a nurse for help. I roll the IV tree while Sara holds her tubing. Seated on the toilet she gripes about this need for assistance. She is disgusted that her eliminations must be measured and tested. And she confides, in dismay, that the staff uses "pee" and "poop" to describe the bodily functions. While I look appropriately shocked, she primly informs me that she has set them straight.

"Have you?" I ask, my eyebrows arching.

"I told them that we prefer the correct terms, Mom. And from now on they should use them."

"What terms, Sara?"

"You know, Mom. The proper ones. 'Whiz' and 'biggie.'"

"Ah, yes," I choke. "The proper ones."

Jeannette, our evening nurse, is waiting outside the bathroom door. As we bump our way back to bed she solemnly announces that she will deal with the whiz and biggie before taking vital signs.

Sara smiles, smug, proud of Jeannette's new-found propriety. I grin, grateful, impressed with Jeannette's innate sensitivity.

While Sara's vital signs are taken, Dr. Baker and Walt shoulder through the doorway. They sit on the end of Sara's bed, back to back, like big bookends.

Dr. Baker wants to perform the spinal tap now and he tells Sara that it will be much easier than the bone-marrow aspiration. She glares at Dr. Baker, and the thermometer juts from her mouth like a naughty tongue.

"Tomorrow," she mumbles.

"Today," he replies.

"Later," she pleads.

"Half hour?" he asks.

"An hour," she counters.

"See you then," he whispers, tweaking her toes.

We talk about the spinal tap and I tell Sara that I had something similar when I delivered her. She asks if it hurt and I tell her I don't remember.

"I was too busy looking forward to meeting you."

"Maybe you could look forward to your next choice from the Red Box," Walt adds.

While we play a few rounds of hangman, Walt watches me, I watch Sara, and Sara watches the clock. The battle for bravery takes it toll.

After the spinal tap, Sara elects to sleep and visit the Red Box in the morning.

The antibiotics are working. Sara's temperature is down,

and as she sleeps she looks all better. We close our eyes tight and pretend to be tucking Sara into her pink gingham quilt at home. A soft knock and a tentative "Hi" bring us back. We walk out of our dream world and into the hallway to sit on the floor with reality, our neighbors Gayle and Rick James.

They are the parents of Erin, twenty-one months old, diagnosed with A.M.L. in March. She is beginning her second course of chemotherapy. Erin is bald, splotchy, scabby-lipped, skinny and scared. Gayle details their past six weeks and I cry and hug this little mama who is not much bigger than the daughter she cradles.

Noses clogged, eyes aching, but finally fresh out of tears, the new neighbors gossip over the fence.

Gayle introduces us to the family across the hall. Three-year-old Billy's A.L.L. is in remission, but he is suffering many side effects from his chemotherapy. His grandparents, his mom and dad and his two sisters are all trying to coax medicine into Billy. His lips are nonexistent. They have been replaced by an oozing black and brown crust.

"Great," I sneer sarcastically to Walt. "Cured of cancer and left lipless for the rest of his life."

While Gayle explains that mouth sores are a common side effect of anti-leukemic drugs, an alarm shrills and a voice on the intercom urges, "Code blue, B-315, code blue, B-315."

In an instant our floor jolts with high voltage. Doctors pop out of the woodwork. Nurses charge after them. Sparks fly from B-315. Billy's room.

The family tumbles into the hallway. Parents moan, sisters wail and grandma prays.

Grandpa shivers when he tells us Billy is having seizures. We all shiver as they wheel Billy rapidly toward intensive care.

The elevator swallows the piping monitors and the weeping family. B-3 waits sullen, quiet, shaken to the core.

We ruffle the muggy calm. Rick shuffles to the lounge for a smoke, Gayle sniffles to the rhythm of her rocking chair, Walt ambles to the snack bar, I blubber away in the shower. And I know for certain that life is more important than lips.

We regroup at shift change to await word of our boy. At midnight we tap the hospital grapevine and learn that Billy will return to the fold soon. He has suffered a stroke but is alert and stable.

Relieved goodnights ripple the stillness and Walt and I are alone with sleeping Sara. We lie tense, close, but separate. We take turns whispering, "This isn't real. This can't be happening to us."

But the *Parents' Handbook on Childhood Cancer* stares up from the night stand and it has our name on it.

Walt wrestles his pillow, attempting to pin down an hour's rest. But I give it up and pad out to read this new bedside bible. I study the "Parental Role," examine "Community Resources" and consider "Financial Arrangements." In the rocking chair my head throbs with "Radiation Therapy," bursts with "Drug Toxicity" and spins from "Unorthodox Treatment."

By the drizzly dawning of Wednesday, May 7, I have memorized the *Parents' Handbook*. I am ready to get on with it.

We squint at the glare from the White Coats. They hunker over clipboards in furtive hallway conference, then file into Sara's room.

She squirms and her lips twitch a perfunctory greeting as

Dr. Baker introduces each member of the hematology staff. But she settles down and meets them head on when he boasts that Sara is B-3's artist in residence.

Dr. Baker chucks Sara's chin, their eyes lock and I wince at the awesome trust she offers him. He snatches it. They banter intimately. The staff fades away, muttering unheard farewells. Finally Dan Baker backs boyish out the door. Sara lies back, lost in love.

I brood on her lingering blush. My head reasons, "Nurture this relationship. It is important to her treatment." I am rational.

My heart warns, "She can't trust him. Nip it in the bud." I am jealous.

My soul whispers, "Wait and watch." I am wary.

Walt fidgets, antsy with unasked, unanswered questions. What are the results of yesterday's spinal tap? When does the chemotherapy begin? He needs to know. He is afraid to ask.

Dr. Baker is frowning into some charts at the nurses' station. He glances up, distracted, when Walt approaches him.

"Are there cancer cells in Sara's central nervous system?"

"Oh. No, Walt. All negative. I should've mentioned that this morning."

Walt and I hug each other, laughing, elated. Dr. Baker looks puzzled. "We really didn't expect to see anything this early. I must not have made that clear," he explains.

But he won't burst our bubble. It is the first positive news we've had since this nightmare began. We pick it up and run with it. The times they are a-changing, Dan Baker. Crazed with euphoria, bold and too loud, I assert that we are ready for Sara's chemotherapy to begin. He carefully eyes me and says that he is working on the dosages. The drugs will arrive tomorrow afternoon. Sara needs a blood transfusion today as her red-blood-cell count is very low. The lab is on the way down to type and cross-match. Maybe, he suggests, we should talk to Sara about it.

She is interested in the transfusion, having watched so many times while Walt and I pumped pints for the Puget Sound Blood Center. She associates bags of blood with sweet ladies who feed her crackers and juice while she waits for us. It is exciting to be on the receiving end—right up until she realizes it involves another arm poke.

Sara fusses and fumes, I cuddle and cluck, the lab tech sticks and sucks.

When it is over, Walt and I kiss our little girl's pouty cheeks and slip away for lunch. Sara sulks. She picks up her pens and paints drippy-lipped vampires and snaggle-toothed Draculas.

In the yellowed, nicotine haze of the cafeteria, between forkfuls of gluey macaroni and cheese, I give Walt his marching orders. And he gives me mine.

In guilty apology, Walt confesses he thinks of home: our son, his school kids, tennis team, district leave policy and our insurance coverage. It is May 7 and our bills aren't paid.

I know what's coming and I'm not surprised. Scared, sad, already lonely, but not surprised.

Walt wonders about going home tomorrow after Sara's chemotherapy begins. He must be with Andy, sort out school commitments and firm up our finances.

I fork patterns in my pudding and expand on Walt's list. Like a teacher in conference, I advise. Andy should spend time with his grandparents, play with his buddies, eat meals at home and sleep in his own bed. Walt should provide security and stability for our boy, even though he has lost it for himself. This child, who thrives on routine and self-destructs without it, must somehow survive. And the "somehow" is Walt.

Andy's daddy scrubs the glaze from his eyes while I preach on. "Talk to people. Make them talk back. They will take their cues from you, be as comfortable as you make them. Be strong and they will return the strength. Will you do it, Walt? Can you do it?"

He grins at the gouges in my pasty pudding. "I will," he affirms with religious fervor, "because the Source of All Knowledge told me to."

And then I cry because I am tired, afraid, out of control, void of faith and not being taken seriously.

Walt scrapes his chair around to my side and apologizes. But he is still laughing. I think What the hell, and I laugh too.

People snake by our table littered with cancer pamphlets. They tsk, nervous, sensing that two flew over the cuckoo's nest. We laugh louder.

Until Walt says, "Listen to me." And he details my job description.

I must be honest always with Sara, yet she must never lose hope. "Tell her the truth, but don't rub her nose in it."

I must make sure she keeps drawing. "Save every scrap, so I don't miss anything."

I must make sure her time is quality time. "Help her find something good in every day."

We bus our dishes and trek down the long fifth-floor corridor to the cadence of an old cliche: "A day at a time . . . make each one count . . . a day at a time . . . make each one count . . . a day at a time . . . make each one count."

And still this is unreal. Not happening to us. It is a soap opera. A grade-B movie. I stop and tilt my ear as I wait for organ music. Or a drum roll. I listen for the emotional plea,

"Let's win this one for the Gipper."

But the elevator inches open to return us to Sara on B-3. The cancer cluster.

The Queen of Sheba holds court. Dark red blood drips into Sara's arm. It beelines to her cheeks. They flush and at least she looks healthy. She is surrounded by chattery new friends.

Mike, the ward clerk, is young, blond and important. He brings the mail and transfers phone calls. Our link to the outside world. Mike elaborately fans a stack of mail, dropping it piece by piece onto Sara's lap. "To Sara, to Sara, to Sara, to Sara." She squeals. It is more mail than she has received in her whole life. Mike hobbles out, kneading his back, muttering about that heavy load of letters.

Laurie, the hematology social worker, leafs through Sara's drawings. She tells Sara about a book nearing completion. It is written for young cancer patients by young cancer patients. Three more illustrations are needed and she thinks she has just located the right artist. Sara's cheeks bloom even brighter as she solemnly accepts the commission. They clinch the deal with a handshake and Laurie leaves. "See ya tomorrow, kiddo!"

Nurse Nancy is off duty, but she lingers, sharing details of her size-seven wedding dress and descriptions of her darling Don. Walt and I smile at the rapture radiating from Sara's whole self. Nancy is a living breathing Barbie Doll.

The transfusion is over, and as Nancy laments the dieting she must do to squeeze into that size seven, she uncouples, then recouples IV tubing. Silently I wish Nancy could plaster her extra pounds onto Sara. For although she is rosy-cheeked, sparkly-eyed and happy, Sara is not hungry. And she grows thinner.

Nancy tootles out the door, promising a picture of Don in the morning. Sara turns to us and gushes girlish, thrilled to be privy to the intimate details of True Love, Snow White and Prince Charming.

While I make our bed and thank God for Nurse Nancy, Sara quiets. She calmly addresses my bent-over backside. "Mom, is leukemia the same as cancer?"

I turn, suddenly sickened, but strangely eager to meet her. I say, "Yes. It is a form of cancer." I catch my breath to go on with the canned speech I have prepared for this moment. But she interrupts and asks, "Do you think we will get invited to Nancy's wedding?"

The evasion tactic was wonderful when used to ward off Dr. Baker, but when Sara employs it on me, Mother Confessor, I am unnerved. In the night I whisper my worries to Walt and we decide to seek counseling from Ralph, the hematology nurse-practitioner.

Wednesday night is nudged by Thursday, and we awaken in stiff-necked anticipation. Chemotherapy begins today. The acceptance of our new reality. Sara has cancer and this is what we are doing about it.

Sara is pensive, tucked inward. Walt is short-fused, with a toddler's attention span. I am uptight and bitchy.

Having dusted and straightened everything except Sara, I attack her next. "Bath time," I command. She balks, then senses my meanness and snaps to.

Bath time is a major undertaking. We gather clean undies, nightie, towels and soap. The newest member of our family, the pump on the rolling IV pole, trails Sara everywhere, regulating the drip of her intravenous feeding. I push it while Sara carries the connecting tubing. In the hall I fashion a cheerful phony face while Sara models a more forthright frown.

I am determined Sara will come clean in the tub room; square up, face facts and assure her mama she is OK.

The tub room is dinky and the three of us are awkward: Sara the pump and I. We clunk across the metal stripping that holds the rug to the cold vinyl floor. Sara rests on the wooden bench while I draw the water. Sullen, she announces she will not undress until I lock the door. With a weary sigh, I concede. She shimmies from her gown, climbs into the tub and lies back, IV arm elevated on the tub's edge. I kneel on the floor beside her.

"Sissy," I say, "today is the day chemotherapy begins."

"I know," she replies.

"It is the medicine that makes you feel worse before you are better."

"I know."

"You may be nauseated and vomit."

"I may not."

"You may have mouth sores."

"I may not."

"The drugs kill fast-growing cells like cancer cells. Hair cells grow fast too and medicine kills them. You may lose your hair."

"Well, I may not," she affirms. But her eyes puddle and so do mine. She lets me scrub her, like I did when she was a baby. Dry her, dress her and cuddle her on my lap. Feeling her heart flutter near mine, I blot out the other possible side effects of Ara-

C and Adriamycin: liver dysfunction, tissue burn and heart damage.

Suddenly Sara pushes off, stands long and lanky, and announces, "I need to feather my bangs while they're still damp. I'll push the pump back myself."

And I know that for this moment Sara has squared up, faced facts and is OK. And it is this moment that counts.

I see her off down the hall, then return to blubber away and disinfect the tub.

On my return trip I find Ralph and Walt just outside Sara's room, perched on colorful child-sized plastic cubes. They are hunched over a pile of paper spread on a tea-party table. I join them, once again impressed that everything about this hospital is child-centered.

Ralph is solemn and short, with a brownish-red beard, and a prematurely receding hairline. He wears a white hospital jacket and his belly strains the buttons. His pockets carry supplies of "puppy stickers." The little dogs wear a gamut of expressions. Each morning, on rounds, the children may choose stickers. Ralph says a child often chooses the puppy face that correlates with the child's own mood. I remember that Sara chose a mad dog this morning.

Ralph is making a calendar of Sara's protocol for Walt to take home. Ralph volunteers little, speaks when spoken to. "Ralph," I begin, pulling up a cube. "We are trying to be honest with Sara, but she changes the subject every time we talk about her disease."

Ralph allows a gentle smile. "We've noticed." He assures us that evasion is a typical means of coping in a child Sara's age. We must continue to present honest information and let Sara decide what to do with it. Ralph adds, "She is very perceptive.

Just be there when she needs you."

Dr. Baker and Craig Jackson, Sara's intern, mosey by and say that the drugs are up. It is time to go for it. We all close in on Sara. Dr. Jackson is a handsome sandy-haired Southern gentleman. With much tenderness he checks Sara's IV site, then gathers her eyes to his and says he must start a new IV for the injection of Adriamycin. She does not wait for explanations. Sara smolders, then explodes, "No, no, no!" She flails her free arm, bringing the sheet over her head.

Dr. Jackson looks to his mentor for help. Craig Jackson is too gentle for this job. Dr. Baker sits by the white heap and says, "Adriamycin will burn tissue if it is injected outside the vein. We need a fresh vein, Sara, so that won't happen."

She jerks from his touch and peers angrily from under the cover. Then, mustering her dignity, she informs the anxious bystanders, "I have to go to the bathroom first. Mom is coming with me."

Regally she leads her mother and the pump through the human obstacle course. Inside the bathroom she whispers, "Lock the door." Then she grabs me around the neck with her good arm, presses her head to my chest and says, "Mama, I've had enough. I don't want to go through with all this. Please. Let's go home with Daddy and forget about this place."

Her desperation startles me. It so accurately mirrors my own. And now it is my turn to muster. Crouched in front of the toilet I hug her tight and tell her what she has to hear.

"Without this medicine, Sara, you will not get well. And as much as I hate for you to hurt, I want you better when we take you home. We are more of a family than ever now. Daddy and Andy will hold down the fort at home and keep it ready for us. You and Mom will go to work on your disease. Together we can handle it. I believe it.''

There is the radiance of innocence and trust on Sara's face. She mumbles, ''I believe it too,'' hitches up her britches, unlocks the door and weaves back to bed.

She whimpers as Dr. Jackson probes her right arm, then uncorks a new vein. Slowly, without breathing, he injects the cherry-Kool Aid-colored Adriamycin. There is a collective exhale when he pulls back the empty syringe. Sara flops back exhausted.

The doctors skulk from our room, anguished. Sara offers no mercy. She's been done dirt. The new IV immobilizes her right arm and hand. Sara can't draw.

Walt brags that he used to be ambidextrous. His daughter scorns him, but I inquire, ''Isn't that usually an inherited trait?''

''Could be,'' Walt answers.

''I'm no good at all left-handed,'' I mourn. ''Sara probably inherited from me.''

She nibbles the bait, picks up a pen and scrawls surreptitiously. ''Wrong!'' she belts. ''I'm Dad's girl. Here's the proof.''

A crude, curly-headed, sourpuss stick figure accompanies shaky but legible printing. ''Sara Beth Kruckeberg, May 8th, lefthanded.''

Cuddled together, father and daughter write and rejoice over their shared specialty. I relax, another hurdle cleared. But not for long.

Chemotherapy begun, Walt is anxious to head for home. He talks to Sara about saving her super lefties and taking care of her mom. She answers she will miss his snoring and asks him to bring back her favorite doll, Big Annie. A hurried hug, a choked-up kiss, and Walt walks away.

At the elevator door, Walt tells me to go back to Sara. He will return Saturday morning with Andy. We cling, I cry, he's gone. So hard to hold up. No place to let down.

Desperate for privacy, I slip into a dark storage room and crumple onto a plastic-covered blue-and-white-ticked mattress. Sobbing silently I wait for the Sign, the Word, the Big Boom from above. But all I hear is Dr. Baker inquiring, "Have you seen Sara's mom?"

I am amused by my new identity. "Here's Sara's mom," I answer, creeping from my hide-out. Dr. Baker asks if everything's OK and I say, "Sure." Together we laugh at his question and my reply. Walking back to the room he says Sara will be violently nauseous in a couple of hours and that he is prescribing Thorazine to sedate her. He will be on call all night if we have any problems.

Sara calls out, "Can I have a hamburger and a chocolate milkshake?"

Dr. Baker says, "Sure, order one up." And I am ecstatic. It is the first food Sara has requested in a week. Maybe, just maybe, she won't be so sick after all.

Sara scarfs down her dinner, then says, "Let's go for a cruise." Because she is immunosuppressed, she must wear a mask for her own protection when she leaves her room. While she ties it on, I find a wheelchair and we are off and rolling. Sara compliments me on my increasing ability to maneuver the wheelchair with one hand and the pump with the other, but she remains terrified of the elevators. The door does not wait for inexperienced mamas, and Sara envisions the elevator ascending with the pump on one side and herself on the other. We are both relieved when we bump onto the fifth floor.

Sara loves the long sloping hallway that leads to the cafeteria and the gift shop. Oh to be rid of the pump and fly free on that gentle incline. Tonight she is content to roll sedately, examining the walls of her favorite floor.

A nursing Pueblo Indian mother, painted in subdued earth tones, greets us as we leave the elevator. Further on Raggedy Ann and Andy tower above us. On the return trip we push uphill to a shady-treed path painted on the end wall.

On the left there are no murals. "What are all these plaques for, Mama?"

"They are hung in memory of people who died and contributed money to this hospital, Sara."

"Did any of them die of cancer?"

"I expect so," I murmur.

"I think it's OK, Mom. You know? What they learned from them helps kids like me. So they didn't die for nothing. Right, Mom?"

"Right, Sara."

A raised eyebrow and a little chuckle, "Just the same, Mama, I'd rather not end up on the wall!"

We laugh too hysterically at Sara's first attempt at gallows humor.

"We'd better head back, Pierre. I'm a little queasy," she announces.

"You and me both," I whisper. "You and me both."

Jeannette welcomes us back to B-3 with thermometer, blood-pressure cuff and a shot of Thorazine. Within thirty minutes, Sara dozes drugged, hanging over the guard rail, vomiting neatly, properly, into the towels on the floor.

Jeannette and I are a team tonight. Hushed efficiency. We work hard. Wiping, washing, changing sheets. Jeannette clucks, "I knew we hadn't seen the last of that burger and shake," and awards me a C– on my hospital corners.

The night watch grieves as Sara moans in and out, "No more Thorazine."

At the 7 a.m. shift change, Nurse Nancy and I guard Sara as she sways on the toilet seat, pointy elbows on knobby knees, hung-over head in hands. "I am so humiliated," she says. "Imagine. An eight-year-old wetting her bed, not once, but three times in the same night. No more Thorazine."

Sara is beat today. She has a bed bath. I read while she rests, clutching the blue emesis bowl under her chin. "Breathe with your mouth closed," she snarls. "You have dog breath."

"I'll brush again." I wince. For the third time. Sara's sense of smell is warped by the chemicals in her system. She orders me to close the door when meal trays are up, says the soap smells moldy and is obsessed with my breath. When I whisper to Nancy that I will be a ventriloquist by the time we leave COH, Sara opens one eye and glowers.

The Ornery One brightens when Mike hauls in her mail. It covers her bed like patchwork. Tucking the bowl under her arm, Sara fans and fingers her booty.

I am amazed at the volume that pours in daily. Mike says he's never seen anything like it. But Sara casually accepts it as an extension of the caring community that has nurtured her since birth. She accepts their love graciously. She has never known anything else. We cuddle their messages around us like a quilt.

Sara smiles off to sleep while I wallpaper the room with her mail. My false front cracks as she drifts off, and I huddle in the rocker at the end of the ward. My false front crumbles clean away when I spy our minister from home. He ambles over, we grip, and blink tears.

And then I pounce. "Where is it, Elmer? The big booming voice from above? Sara believes in angels, Elmer. Father, Son and Holy Ghost. Our Father, who art in heaven. Sara believes. Well, why haven't we heard from Good Old God, Elmer? Why?"

He shrugs, tugs at his billy-goat beard. He rubs his eyes behind thick lenses. "What does hold you together, Carol? Keeps you on your feet?"

"The phone calls. The letters. Our family. Our friends. They shoulder in close. And sometimes they lift us above it all. That's what."

"Maybe there's your big booming voice. Worth considering anyway."

Sara and I settle in to 6 a.m. blood draws, 9 a.m. tub times and morning sickness twenty-four hours a day.

Uncle Bill brings homemade pizza Friday night and Sara banishes us from her room. We settle on the floor outside the door. "It still stinks," she bellows. "Clear out completely."

We skulk to the "living room" at the end of the hall. My little brother is so sad—she is *his* Sara too. He taught her to give the raspberries with a mouth full of Gerbers, to belch at will, to cup her hand under her armpit and fire off rude noises. She loves his grossness. He loves her propriety. She calls him Uncle Bull. He calls her Little Lady.

No longer able to buck up, I wail. "Oh, Bill. Why didn't we take life seriously when we had the chance? Appreciate it. Cherish it." Bubble-brained, laughing at our own jokes, we lived life on the surface. Maybe, just maybe, if we'd knuckled under, we wouldn't have been brought up so short. I think about the poem Bill découpaged for me. It hangs by the phone in my kitchen.

> Isn't life lovely?
> Isn't life gay?
> Isn't life the perfect way
> To pass the time away?

What a fool I was to fall for it.

We talk about tomorrow when Walt will return with Andy and Mom and Dad. They will stay at Bill's in Tacoma. Bill says he will do anything to help. And I believe him.

On the way to the elevator, Bill bids Sara farewell with a few armpit freeps. She scowls, "Oh, Uncle Bull!" And burps in his face.

"Little Lady!" he roars, and leaves laughing with tears on his cheeks.

Another endless night. We put Sara on a bedpan every hour to eliminate the fluids flushing through her. But it's all worth it. In the morning she grins, glad to be dry, yawns, and asks if Andy will arrive early enough for Saturday-morning cartoons.

After her bath, Sara powders and perfumes, tidies her table and wraps hospital goodies as treasures for Andy. Unable to sit tight any longer, we grab the blue bowl and a couple of books and wheel up to the fourth floor to watch the parking-lot entrance.

I wait silently, studying the cover of my book, *The World According To Garp*. I think of Garp's Undertoad, and I know it's got me by the innards.

Sara waits silently, studying the cover of her book, *Little House in the Big Woods*. She thinks of Laura's pioneer philosophy and she touches my arm and lays it on. "'Make hay while the sun shines,' Mama. That's how we'll do it."

When the troops arrive from the home front, we spend the morning sharing forced smiles, opening gifts from friends and almost containing Andy.

Sara slides into new red satiny pj's with quilted yoke and lace trim. She wears them like a trademark. As I tie red yarn in her hair, I smile. Smug. Every morning I fluff out Sara's long curly hair, then furtively examine the hairbrush. So far, so good. Not a strand shed. It's very possible these doctors don't know everything.

Sara rests, serene. Grandpa reads to her, massages her hand. Grandma memorizes her, studies her face.

Walt and I trail Andy to the cafeteria for lunch and together time. The teacher in me demands that I educate Andy. He must know what's coming down.

"Andy," I smile, "we need to talk about Sara's disease so that you understand why our family must be separated for a while."

He whips up his right hand, a traffic policeman, peers out over his chocolate-milk mustache and commands, "Stop. Dad already telled to me all of this. Sara's got zuchinnia. I can't catch it. This is the only place that can help her. I don't want her to be alone so it's OK for you to stay. Don't talk about it any more. Who is sicker? Sara or Ahmed?''

Ahmed is a black ten-year-old with brain cancer. Andy met him this morning in the playroom. Ahmed slumps, slurs, drools and is almost bald. Ahmed frightens Andy.

"Their cancers are different," I assure my son and myself. "Sara may lose her hair like Ahmed, but the rest of her will stay the same."

"I don't want her bald," he pleads. "I'll be embarrassed."

"Andy!" I plead. "Don't you ever say that to Sissy. . . ." I want to smack him and hug him tight all at the same time. He marches to the elevator. He is too big, too bold, too brassy.

Walt and I trudge after him. We don't speak because we have no answers.

Mama meets us at the desk. "Look who's here!" she greets.

A slender, suntanned, wire-haired will-of-the-wisp bebops into my outstretched arms. She is Sue. My best friend. My confidante. The idol of my childhood. She is electric. B-3 clicks on. Colors burst brilliant. Sounds clarify. Sara tingles. The whole world focuses on Sue.

It is 1954. I am eight. Sue is nine. It's the first day of school in a brand-new city. I am alone on the playground, very sick from being very scared. Sue sweeps by, in charge, hands me the end of a jump rope and commands, "Turn." Life goes on. Sue sees to it.

We spend the afternoon catching up and recollecting. Sue graduated from the University of Washington School of Nursing. She was a hematology nurse right here on B-3 until five years ago when she gave birth to her daughter, Carrie.

While Andy and Carrie fall in love in the hallway, Sue and I entertain wide-eyed Sara with tales of our girlhood.

Sue threw a dart that missed the board and lodged in my stomach next to my appendix scar. While she pulled it out she twisted my arm and made me swear never to tell. I kept the secret until today, twenty-six years later.

Sue wore her father's 42-long tuxedo. I wore her sister's D-cup strapless net formal and we pretended to go to the prom. Sue brought down a great "fur" coat from the attic and smothered it around my shoulders. A big hunk of Fiberglas insulation. Then I had to suffer the indignity of Sue's big brother Dave tweezing glass from my back while I whimpered naked in the tub. Sue looked so guilty I only loved her more.

Sue and I built a go-cart and waited for the power lawnmower to sail us down Seventeenth Street. When it didn't, we junked it and skated Couples Only at the Armory.

Sue won the sense-of-humor valentine at Bellingham High School three years straight. I cheered the loudest.

Too soon, Sue prepares to "buzz off." She links her arm in mine and says, "I live five minutes from the hospital. I am your wheels. I am your laundress. I am your psychiatrist. I am whatever you need me to be. I am your best friend again. See you tomorrow, Carol the Barrel."

And while I watch her sashay out the door, I remember us galloping around the lake, horse and rider all in one, slapping our thighs, shouting, "Hyah, hyah!" Sara sees my smile and says, "Must be a good one, Mom. Tell me about it."

I say a silent thank-you prayer. My Sara has met my Sue. Sue swept by, assessed our situation and commanded, "Turn." Life goes on. Sue sees to it.

The weekend crashes to a close. It hurts so bad hugging my little boy goodbye. He loves Grandma and Grandpa, but he wants to play in his own yard, rock in his own rocking chair. Be with his own dog. And his own mom. He whimpers it in my ear. His tears smear my cheek. His nose smudges my neck.

Walt hoists him away, squeezing him with a gentle reminder. "I know," whimpers Andy. "It's my job to be good for Grammy and to not make Mama more sad."

A large task for a small child. One last kiss for my boys and they race off to catch the ferry.

Time ticks on for the creatures of routine.

Every day at 6:00 a.m., a lab technician tiptoes in for the daily blood draw. Sara is mean in the morning. And to wake to the vampire is obscene. I climb onto her bed each day to see her through the pokes.

Every day at 6:45, an intern arrives to perform Sara's examination. COH is a teaching institution. Interns rotate through B-3, with a new one assigned to Sara every three weeks. I love their youth, their intensity, their total dedication to my daughter.

Every day at 7:00, a day-shift nurse, usually Nancy, shuffles in to take vitals. Nancy is nasty in the morning, lurching around on automatic pilot, a woman of few words until after her coffee break. We speak the same silent language, Nancy, Sara and I.

Every day at 7:30 the breakfast tray rattles into the room. Sara surveys it, gags, then switches on the TV. I growl into the bathroom to get dressed. "I want that juice gone by the time I'm out." She pierces me with her sour hospital face. But the juice has been swilled down when I reappear. I coax, threaten and bribe a little more breakfast into Sara, then help her brush her teeth and swish Nystatin, a rinse to help prevent mouth sores. She hates it, but uses it faithfully, insisting she will never have mouth sores.

Every day at 8:30, Henrietta Hippo fills the seven-inch TV screen announcing, off key, "The New Zoo Revue." Sara grins, "See you later, Mom. Have a good breakfast." I can't escape fast enough.

Every day I climb the back stairs to the fifth floor. I meet Dr. Pendergrass between the third and fourth floors. He asks, "How goes it?" and I answer, "Pretty good."

Every day I buy a morning newspaper from the machine outside the cafeteria. And the same intern sneaks a freebie before the lid snaps shut.

Every day I buy grapefruit juice, bagel with cream cheese and coffee with cream and sugar. The red-haired cashier asks, "How's Sara this morning?" And I answer, "Pretty good."

Every day I sit at the back table on the left side by the window and eat my breakfast, reading the front section of the paper. Then at 9:00 I take the back stairs down to B-3 to sit on my bed and read the rest.

At 9:30 it's bath time. If Sara's counts are high enough, we troop down to the tub room. If her counts are low, we have a bed bath. Sara dons the "negligée of the day" and waits in her wheelchair while I tackle the bed change.

By 10:00 we are ready for rounds. The cluster of hematologists, residents, interns, nurses and therapists hover outside our closed door while our intern discusses Sara's course of treatment. After a brief exchange, they herd in for a visit. If Sara wears her red satins, Dr. Pendergrass sings "The Lady in Red." If she wears the Miss Piggy nightshirt, he oinks. For her other gowns, he merely wolf-whistles.

We spend the rest of the morning cruising, drawing, playing games or reading.

At noon we worry over the lunch tray. I leave, exasperated, to hike the stairs for my chef's salad with three cherry tomatoes on top.

I zip back for the highlight of our day—the mail. No matter how sick Sara feels, she perks up for her letters and packages.

"Kristen is my faithful friend," sighs Sara. "She writes every day."

"She learned that from her mama," I say, opening my

letter from Kristen's mama, Carol. Physically warmed. Mentally uplifted.

Sara naps after lunch, wrapped in this blanket of love from home. I write letters, read cancer information or play with a kid whose mom is gone.

Three o'clock is shift change. If Sara feels up to it, we work on some rude trick to perform for Adrian when he comes around for vital signs. Sara loves to hold her breath while Adrian checks her respiration. Depending on counts, we visit rec-therapy or play in our room until dinner at 5:00.

Another meal, same old battle. I am a mama. Good appetite means good health. I am obsessed with Sara's eating habits. She craves salty chips and sugary pop. No matter how many times I am told that this is normal behavior for chemotherapy patients, it's all wrong to me. And I will never accept it as OK.

I make my last trip upstairs for supper. An hour later I won't remember what I ate. I wind weary back home for an evening of TV and good talk.

I settle Sara by 10:00 and wait in line for my shower. Though my heart belongs to my bathtub in Sequim, I am always eager for the evening shower. The parents' shower room is tiny, with a mirror on the back of the door and a bench in the corner. The hand-held shower head is always pointed the wrong way and I get it in the ear every night. In the shower I can shout at injustice, bargain with God and blubber to myself. But eventually I must hop out, dry off and smile on out the door.

The games, books and Barbie Dolls are put away. Johnny's monologue is over. It's dark. The IV pump hums, the clock ticks, and Sara comes alive. Nurse Karen calls it our slumber party. Sara and I ponder love and hate, good and evil. Living and dying.

Sara's initial infusion ends tonight, Wednesday, May 14. We eagerly watch the last bag of Ara-C drip into Sara's thin, bruised vein.

Dr. Baker bounces in for the ceremonial removal of the IV needle, then drops a bomb. "If you drink like a son-of-a-gun, and maintain a normal temp over the next couple of days, Sara, we'll kick you outta here."

The skinny skeptic fisheyes the shaggy doctor. "Friday?" she queries. "This Friday? Day after tomorrow Friday?"

"Sounds good." He tugs her toes, and tootloos out the door. Sara flies high. I am floored. He never told us we'd be sent away between infusions. This room is our home, B-3 our neighborhood, these people our family, our friends. I've worked hard to make it that way. How dare this big, bearded bearer of glad tidings give us the boot?

"Call Daddy and Andy," Sara smiles. "I'll spill 'em the beans."

"In a little bit, Sissy," I mumble. "I'm going to find Dr. Baker and ask him a thing or two."

More like tell him a thing or two!

Huffing down the hall, I snag Dr. Baker and get him into a conference room and demand an explanation for this new twist. Dumbstruck, he studies my distress, then reads me right and sweet-talks. "I know you're afraid, Carol. But remember? In the beginning you and Walt indicated you wanted as much normal family time as possible with Sara. That's why we're letting her go home for a week. Don't worry. Your pediatrician will do daily blood checks. You'll watch her closely for infection, since her counts are decreasing. But the important part is you'll all be home together. And that's good, huh?''

When he looks at me like a little boy eager to please, my school-teacher posture cracks. And when he touches my shoulder it crumples all to pieces.

"It's OK to run scared. It's OK," soothes Dan Baker. "It's OK."

And while he talks, I think of home: tucking in my Andy Boy, winding his Winnie mobile "one more time, please," cooking a meal my Sara might eat, sleeping under my own quilt with my own Walt. Maybe, just maybe, it will be OK.

Dr. Baker says, "Get some sleep. You look beat."

"You don't look so hot yourself." I grin. He was on the floor at 6:30 this morning. It's hours past supper and here he sits, comforting Nervous Nellie. Maybe, just maybe, Dan Baker is OK too.

Sara drinks like a son-of-a-gun and runs no fever. Friday morning we get a final go-ahead and begin to pack up. When our room is stripped of cards, pictures and toys, we don't belong here any more. But it's harder to get out than it was to get in. While we wait for a physician to sign our release and another to give us outpatient orders, we rub each other raw.

"Let's get this show on the road—*now*," Sara crabs for the eighty-first time.

"This hospital does not revolve around you, Sara Beth," I snap. "Walt, you could conceivably get off your duff and see what's taking so long."

"Relax," he croons in that I'm-dealing-with-a-little-child voice. "We'll get home today."

"Easy for you to say," I snarl. "You didn't spend three hours tearing this room apart, boxing up all this stuff."

"Right. I had a leisurely morning getting lesson plans to school and Andy to Grandma's house by seven. Why didn't you find out exactly when she'd be released before you insisted I get here at the crack of dawn?"

"Great. Lay it all on me, Walt. It's all my fault you didn't get your twelve-hour beauty rest. You think you're tired! You don't know what tired is. . . ."

Walt stomps into the hall in search of his cool and smacks into Dr. Baker who chirps, "Fly away home. Blood checks daily. Continue the mouth care. Call the pediatrician if Sara's temp goes over 100°, or if she's bruising or bleeding. Keep her fairly isolated. Relax and have a great week."

We teeter away from COH, fledglings pushed from the nest. On the ferryboat, Sara rolls down the car window and sniffs in the sea-salty breeze. "Free at last," she giggles. And we all hug. Heading home feels good.

Sara wobbles into Grandma and Grandpa's house. They hug her gingerly, heads turned away, afraid of infecting her with unseen germs. Andy has no such qualms. He laps around his sister, a puppy dog greeting a long-lost master.

Grandma says she spiffed up our house a bit, and she hopes that's all right. I give her a squeeze. Walt, Sara, Andy and I load into the car, glad to be four again.

Our front door is a giant greeting card: WELCOME HOME SARA! Newly planted pansies smile outside Sara's bedroom window, and neighbors hang over their fences, gate-to-gate happy faces. Dinner in the oven, roses on the table, champagne in the fridge. Here's to Dr. Baker! The important part is we're all home together.

Saturday morning Walt and I lie snuggled up tight, eavesdropping on the cuddling and cajoling, the giving and taking, the living and loving that drifts from down the hall. The kids are up. And for the moment, it's any old Saturday morning. I close my eyes and remember the beginning of their love affair.

"Our new baby is a work of art," boasted Andy's birth announcement. The artist's depiction of our new boy was, itself, a masterpiece. She had captured his bold broad body, interpreted his google-eyed grin, portrayed his perfection. And she was only three years old!

We recognized her gift the first time she fisted a fat primer crayon. Now Sara's talent would be known nationwide as she announced the birth of her brother, the baby she called our "joy boy."

Eagerly I awaited the onset of sibling rivalry, for I was properly "Spocked" on its treatment. But it was never to be.

She was so easily seduced by that snappy, happy-go-lucky chuckler, the perfect foil for herself, our serious, sensitive first-born. Andy's early-morning crowing brought her cribside, sleep-swollen and lion-maned, where she doted on his obvious delight at the presence of his Sissy-girl. A precedent was set, and for five years, sunrises belonged to Sara and Andy.

We puffed prideful when the world became wise to their early-morning escapades. On open-house night we visited the new elementary-school library an embarrassing number of times to admire eight-year-old Sara's latest portrait of Andy. And its accompanying poem:

Little Brothers

Sara Beth Kruckeberg

Little brothers are absurd,
In the morning they sound like an elephant herd.
They wake you up too early,
And then mess up your hair,

Sometimes I think that mine acts
Just exactly like a bear.
But mostly he is just right,
He laughs and rides his bike,
And I am glad to have him,
He's a kid I like.

Andy had pondered then pouted over that last line. He de-
manded to know why it did not read, "He's a kid I love." I
sailed into an overblown philosophical explanation on the na-
tures of "like" and "love," summarizing that, in many in-
stances, liking might be preferable to loving. My sermon completed, Andy looked bewildered. He grinned and relaxed, however, when Sara nudged him and whispered, "Besides all that,
Andy, 'like' rhymes with 'bike.'"

And now, one more time, the joy boy and his Sissy-girl
share the sunrise.

Andy varooms into our bedroom to report that Sissy is
droopy, so he poured her cereal. She whispers in behind him,
wrapped in her rabbit quilt, and asks her daddy to make the traditional Saturday-morning doughnut run.

Her wish is his command. Walt is dressed, shaved,
brushed and out the door in ten minutes. Sara agrees to a bath
while we await the chocolate-covered, custard-filled goodies.

As the water runs, Andy arrives at tub's edge, stripped,
with an armload of rubber dinosaurs. He's ready to hop in with
Sara, the way he always has.

"You can't bathe with Sissy," I explain. "She might pick
up a germ from you."

"Choose first, Sara," Andy says, ignoring me, thrusting

the prehistorics at his sister.

"Didn't you hear Mama? Get out of here," she snips.

He chucks his biggest brontosaurus at her and bawls out of the bathroom.

"Let me pile your hair on top of your head, Sara," I sigh. "Then pop in while I talk to Andy."

"Be careful," she warns. "There's a huge tangle in my hair."

"There sure is," I say, pulling the brush through the sunny brown curls that reach to the middle of her back. By the end of that first stroke, the huge tangle is gone. It wafts clingy down my nightgown, then settles on the blue carpet.

"Oh Sara," I gasp.

"Oh Mama," she cries. She grabs the brush and jerks it through her hair over and over again. Great gobs of hair chunk loose, covering the counter, the sink, the toilet seat, the floor. Hair. Everywhere.

And although we've denied that this could happen to us, inside our secret selves we have prepared, Sara and I.

"They weren't just a-woofin', were they Mama?"

"I guess not, Sissy-girl," I mutter. "Why don't you get into the bathtub and we'll shampoo the rest of the loose stuff out."

"I don't think all of my hair will fall out. Do you, Mom?"

"No," I confirm. "It'll just thin a bit, probably."

Sara and I may be prepared, but Andy stands naked in the doorway, aghast at the carnage. Quiet little tears trickle down his big baby cheeks. I leave Sara alone to weep with my little boy.

Walt returns, surveys the scene, and we all find it hard to choke down those doughnuts.

Sara gives Saturday cartoons absolute concentration. She continues to brush, silent, obsessive, making neat nests of her fallen hair. Her brushing stops midstroke when a commercial for St. Jude's Research Hospital announces, "Our children are dying of cancer . . ."

And Sara asks quietly, "Are children dying of my kind of cancer?"

And I answer, more quietly, "Some are . . ."

And Andy interrupts, "But not you, Sissy. Not you."

Sara smiles her grandma smile, pats his head and brushes some more.

Sunday morning, May 18, is bacon and eggs, cinnamon toast, and trying not to notice lost hair flying all around the breakfast table.

Walt, grey-skinned, puffy-eyed; Andy, rosy-cheeked, wild-eyed; Sara, pasty-faced and sad-eyed, tolerate my phony Susie Homemaker good cheer. Barely. I am squeaky new shoes on blistered old feet. I hate the sound of myself but I can't shut up. We must not give up this early in the game.

The table shivers, the windows shimmy, the horizon rumbles and the sullen little family explodes.

"What was that?" Sara tremors.

"Bombs away!" Andy blasts.

"I don't know," Walt erupts, running out the back door. We charge behind, standing in our pj's on the back porch. The neighbors join Walt in the alley.

"Blasting in Happy Valley," assures Mr. Cole.

"Tanker truck explosion on the highway?" guesses Mrs. Sampson.

"Damned jets foolin' around with the sound barrier.

Ought to be a law," growls the neighborhood Mr. Crab.

"Mount Saint Helens?" I venture. They snort. They scoff. They jeer. And the more they deride, the more righteous I become. The paper boy pedals by shouting, "Volcano blew!" They laugh at the kid too.

We saunter back into the house, the children and Walt arm in arm, getting their jollies heehawing old Mom.

Lord, how I love it when CBS "Sunday Morning" is interrupted "so that we may bring you a special news bulletin. Mount Saint Helens in Washington State is in the process of a major eruption. We will bring you further details as they develop."

The phone rings all afternoon. Friends and relatives want to chat about catastrophies; the one at 226 Matriotti Avenue, Sequim, and the one in Southwest Washington. Over and over my family listens as I reiterate that Sara is under treatment at one of the best places in the world for childhood cancer. Walt, Sara and Andy roll their eyes and shake their heads at one another when I zip into the Mount Saint Helens saga. My story gets louder and better with each telling.

We laze around the TV set all afternoon, caught up in this new crisis. I harbor a guilty gladness about the devastating volcano.

It gives us a new focus: ashfall instead of hairfall.

It gives us a new perspective: we are a small speck in all of creation.

It gives us gut knowledge: we are not in the driver's seat.

And when I study my balding little speck who's just along for the ride, I am very afraid. She is sleeping flushed, breathing fast. With a sense of "What now?" I insert the thermometer.

Monday morning Sara is a lion. She wakes, pawing strands of fallen mane from her pillow, spitting hair from her mouth. She lashes at her keepers and roars from the bath. "I don't want to go to Port Angeles again. I only want to sleep."

Dr. Turner, our pediatrician, wants to keep tabs on Sara's slight fever and the effect of his prescribed antibiotics. Sara's blood work must also be done.

Mom drives us in, working hard at cheery chit chat. Sara lies limp in the back seat, moaning, "Oh Grandma. You'll never get all this hair out of your new car."

"Don't worry, Sissy," soothes Grandma, "It's Grandpa's job to clean the car!"

We use the back entrance to the clinic so Sara won't have to sit in a germy waiting area. The nurse directs us to a room and shuts the door. Sara cuddles her head in my lap. Her cheeks are dry and hot.

Dr. Turner edges in, assesses us, then musters his best bedside manner. Casually, he rolls his stool up next to Sara, touches her forehead and slides off her scarf. She snatches it back, slits her rheumy eyes, curls her lip and snarls.

"Shape up, Sara," I warn. "He's only doing what he has to do."

She clutches the scarf to her head, digs in deeper. Dr. Turner says, "Come on, Sara. I need you up on the table." She closes her eyes and snugs farther into my lap.

I am bewildered. Do I take his part against her? Or do I hang with my little girl? Her only ally. Dr. Turner knows I can't push her away and he examines her on my lap, the way he did when she was a baby.

After the blood draw, the nurse slaps a Mickey Mouse Band-Aid on Sara's arm. She grins and reports, "They just have plain ones at my hospital."

"Whoopee!" shouts Dr. Turner. "We've scooped COH!"

Dr. Turner says he will call us with Sara's counts after he telephones them to Seattle. We are to keep watch on the fever.

Sara drinks an A & W root beer, then drifts away the afternoon, spirit drooping, temperature rising. By the time Dr. Turner calls, I am a wreck. The doctor listens to my report: "Sara is depressed, listless and feverish," then gives me his: "Her counts have bottomed out," and we reach agreement. Sara must return to COH. He will call to make arrangements.

Before leaving for Seattle, we backtrack to the clinic so that Sara can be injected with the antibiotics prescribed by the hematologists.

We wrench ourselves from Andy, left against his will at Grandma's house, deposit Walt's lesson plans at school, pack up a suitcase and speed down Highway 101.

Sara sleeps hard while I talk low. I hate the relief rushing through me. But home was horrible. The watching. The waiting. The need to be doctor and nurse, minister and friend, wife and mother. Everything to everybody. Walt whispers what I want to hear, "I understand, and it's OK."

Three hours later, we three hold hands as we head up the hill to our hospital. Admissions is waiting, and Sara settles in to 313. She perks up and I know that she, too, is relieved to be back.

"The little bugger didn't trust me to do it all right," I fume.

"Smart cookie," laughs Walt.

Dr. Baker and Dr. Jackson breeze in for the admit exam and Sara greets them as long-lost relatives. Nobody notices Sara's balding head, so she mentions it herself. "Grandma gave me this blue hair net so my hair won't fall all over the bed."

"Great idea," says Craig Jackson. "You look good in blue."

"Did you bring those snazzy red satins?" says Dan Baker.

"I'll wear them tomorrow," she says and blushes.

We have a new neighbor: a chunky, fuzzy-haired, two-year-old sweetheart, Lynsey Hunter. Cozied in clown sleepers, she peek-a-boos into our hearts, then buries her face in her little mama's tanned shoulder.

Becky Hunter is a ninety-pound bundle of nervous energy. She accepts my greeting with a tight nod, a grim smile and a blunt pronouncement: "We're here from Ohio for a bone-marrow transplant. And I'm not going to get involved here with all these kids. I just can't take it any more. If you get my drift."

"Who's Lynsey's donor?" I ask, ignoring her warning.

"Our four-year-old, Olivia. She'd like to meet your Sara, if that's OK."

"Sure. Come over whenever . . ." But beware, Becky Hunter. If you meet my Sara, you're done for. Involved. If you get my drift.

Somewhere in his ravings, Dan Baker had mentioned a bone-marrow transplant. The closest thing to a cure for A.M.L.? An experimental treatment? Possibility unlikely? Risky? Premature to discuss it? Just what did he say? I'll corner him on rounds tomorrow.

A seed of hope. Planted by the Hunters of Ohio.

This morning Sara is glued to "The Wizard of Oz," playing on the COH closed-circuit Geni station. I sit on the hallway heater vents with Dan Baker. I want to know all there is to know about bone-marrow transplants. I am eager. He is reticent. I am forthright. He is evasive. I am angry. And he is stubborn.

"It's way too early to talk transplant," he says. "In the first place, it's an unlikely possibility. In the second place, we haven't even achieved a remission. Don't think too far ahead."

"That's easy for you to say," I argue. "I want to learn about something that might keep my daughter alive. And you tell me I shouldn't think about it?"

"You're just building yourself up for a fall, Carol." I don't answer Dan Baker, because if I speak, I'll cry. I want him to see me as a mature, in-control equal, not a blubbering, hysterical housewife. He's got to know that I can handle whatever he dishes out. All the facts, not just what he chooses to spoon-feed.

"By the way, it's time for a mid-course aspiration. This time we also want a biopsy. We'll scrape some solid marrow off the inside of the bone. Sara can have an anesthetic so she won't remember it. Gotta run. I'll be in to talk to Sara this afternoon."

When I join Sara, she is carefully examining her gums in the bed-tray mirror, under the watchful eye of Nurse Nancy.

"They're bleeding, Nancy. I brushed too hard."

"Maybe, Sara. But your platelets are low, too. We're going to transfuse you with some today."

"No more pokes!" Sara wails.

Nancy to the rescue. "Cool it, Sara. Your IV is still good. You won't need another stick."

"Promise?"

"Promise."

Big cheerful grin. "Care for a cruise, Mama?" she invites. "Before we're stuck here all afternoon?"

We hit the high spots; the infant-care unit, first-floor snack bar, fifth-floor gift shop, and the sixth-floor hematology clinic. In the elevators, Sara studies doctors, jokes with "vampires," compliments cleaning ladies and meets dieticians. They know her from the drawings she doodles on her menus. "Anything you want, Sara. You just let us know."

Sara grins behind the mask, adjusts her scarf and I feel this crazy, unexpected warmth of well-being. I don't understand it, but I grab it.

The platelets are up when we return to the floor. The plastic bag full of cream-colored opaque lifesavers are hooked up to Sara's IV. As they infuse, we play our favorite card game, Uno, and talk wigs.

At shift change, Sara is irritable. "What a sore loser," I say. She pouts, rubbing her scarf back and forth over her scalp. "Does just talking about a wig make your head itch?" I venture.

"I itch all over and I'm steaming hot," Sara says. Red splotches welt all over her head and face. And before our eyes, they spread down her chest and arms. I race into the hall to get Jeannette.

Sara is having an allergic reaction to the platelets, a fairly common occurrence, soothes our nurse. Sara is given Benadryl and within fifteen minutes the hives subside and she drifts off.

"I hate sleeping," she slurs. "Get the name of that platelet donor. We won't use him again."

"Such a funny little sweetheart," Jeannette whispers. "I'd like one just like her."

While Sara sleeps, Patti Trull visits with a list of children's wig outlets. Patti is pretty, cheerful, sensitive and a cancer survivor. Twelves years ago, at fifteen, Patti lost her leg to osteogenic sarcoma. She is supposed to be our cancer rehabilitation therapist, but at this point she is just a hank of long, thick, luxurious hair. Proof positive that Sara, too, will grow new hair. Perhaps even more beautiful than before.

"Don't spend a lot of money," counsels Patti, "until you're sure Sara will wear a wig."

"We want her to at least have the option. We can afford it," I assure Patti. "Besides, it's something tangible I can do for Sara. You know, therapy for the mother."

"Go for it," laughs Patti, leaving me alone with the phone.

After several calls, I settle on the Chic Coiffures, make an appointment for the consultation, call Sue's taxi service and arrange for a pickup tomorrow afternoon.

When Sara stirs, I tell her the exciting news. "Just so it looks exactly like my old hair," she warns.

"We'll discuss that when you're brighter-eyed," I hedge.

Sara suffers a drug hangover. She is mean and weepy when Dr. Baker tells her about the biopsy.

"But Sissy," I explain, "at least it won't hurt you. You'll just sleep through it."

"Mama, I hate sleeping," Sara sobs.

"Why do you hate sleeping?" Dr. Baker asks softly.

Sara hides her face in a pillow. Her reasons remain her own.

Dr. Baker slaps his knees, exhales the hair off his brow, stands, then slumps out the door.

Sara lies very still until her dinner tray arrives. She eats a few bites of turkey, plain mashed potatoes, four green beans and drinks all of her milk. She asks for a popsicle from the nutrition room, and I coax her into walking with me to choose one. She won't go to rec-therapy tonight, preferring to draw in her room. While the orange popsicle melts in its wrapper, I head for the shower.

When I return, Sara shares her masterpiece. She has pasteled a picture of a gentle-faced Jesus, surrounded by white-nightied, angel-winged cherubs. In elaborate cursive, Sara has penned, "The Golden Gates of Heaven. Jesus Is With Us."

The sight of it sickens me. Sara senses it, offers a maternal pat and grins wry, "Don't worry, Mama. None of these kids are me. See? They've all got hair on their heads!"

"It's really pretty, Sissy. Do you think that's the way it really is?"

"God only knows," she sighs. We catch her joke simultaneously and laugh away the tensions of the day.

After mouth care and long-distance goodnight kisses for Daddy and Andy, Sara and I settle in the dark for the inevitable chat.

She waits a long time and I think she's fallen asleep. Then, in a whisper, "Mama, what happens when you die?"

"Well," I blunder. "I know about the body, but I'm not positive about the soul."

"Tell me about the body then."

"OK. The body is taken to a funeral home where it's cared for until it's buried or cremated."

"What's cremated?"

"That's when the body is incinerated and then the family may bury, scatter or do whatever with the ashes. That's probably what Daddy and I want done when we die."

"Not me," Sara interrupts. "I want to be buried whole. In that park where Mrs. Dunn is buried. What happens at a funeral?"

"Well, some people have the body in the casket at the funeral and some people have a memorial service with the body already gone. The minister tells what was special about the person who died and helps the people who are left behind feel better. There are beautiful flowers at a funeral sometimes and other times the family requests that instead of flowers, friends give money to a charity. That's probably what Daddy and I want done when we die."

"Not me," affirms Sara. "I would like a memorial service with lots of flowers. I love roses."

"I know you do," I mumble.

Sara plumps her pillow with a "that's that" thump and says, "Let's play 'what was good about today.' You go first."

"OK," I answer, glad to be done with dying. "It was watching you pork out on those green beans."

She laughs that big laugh that makes me feel like a cross between Erma Bombeck and Phyllis Diller, then shares her favorite part of the day. "It was the mail again, Mama. I'm the luckiest buck in the world to have a whole city of friends."

Quiet. Then a drowsy, "Good night, sleep tight, don't let the bedbugs bite."

"And if they do, take your shoe, and beat 'em black and blue," I answer. Proud to be the mom of the luckiest buck in the world.

But Sara throws craps in the morning. Dr. Baker and Dr. Jackson tell her about the anesthetic Nurse Nancy is injecting into her vein.

"We're gonna find out what kind of a drunk you are, Sara. This medicine makes you a little tipsy. You'll be sleepy but you won't hurt. You won't remember anything when you wake up in a couple of hours. You'll be awake for lunch," says Craig Jackson.

"Whoopee," Sara mutters.

"We'll get the treatment room ready and be right back for you. Don't run off," jokes Dr. Dan.

Sara stares them out the door, then pets my arm. "Don't ever leave me, Mama."

"Never," I promise.

She begins to phase out, but weaves in to grin silly with wavery unfocused eyes. When the physicians return, she giggles, "A word of praise is never wasted. Leave my underpants on. I mean it."

"I just knew Sara'd be a funny drunk," drawls Dr. Jackson. They roll her onto the treatment table and wheel her away. She smiles, a Cheshire cat, as I scurry along beside her.

In the treatment room, Sara moans during the aspiration,

but seems to be asleep. So much easier than the last time.

And then the horror of the biopsy begins.

"OK, Craig," coaches Dr. Baker. "To get the scrape you've really got to use some force. Push down until you can't go any further, then really rock it."

Hold the phone. "It" is my daughter's skinny little body. But Dr. Jackson follows orders. The table scoots as Sara rolls back and forth, back and forth. Her eyes open and she gasps from deep inside. From her marrow.

Stop it right now. Right now!

Dr. Baker says, "Good. Now rock it the other way." And the kind, gentle Craig Jackson muscles into it. The table scoots again as Sara rolls up and down, up and down. I lay my head near Sara's head and muffle her noises into my wet cheek.

"It's over, Mrs. Kruckeberg," breathes Dr. Jackson.

"All done, Sara," booms Dr. Baker. "How ya doin'?"

"Fine," she woozes, then offers a smitten smile and sleeps deep.

"Sweet Sara," sighs Craig Jackson. And I forgive him.

But not you, Dr. Dan. Giver of the orders. Never you. Today I hate you.

Sara wakes wounded. She needs to potty but refuses the bedpan. "I'll pee in the hat," she scowls, lapsing into hospital slang. When her feet hit the floor, Sara whimpers with pain. She winces her way to the bathroom, drops her drawers, and eases onto the toilet. She slaps away the tissue and sympathy I offer.

"I'll wait outside," I say. "Call if you need me."

"I'm sorry, Mama. Don't leave me. I'm just mad because they got blood on my best underwear," she sobs, staring at the Carter size tens drooped around her ankles.

"I'll buy you new ones," I offer. "Slippery ones? Bikini ones?"

"Black ones?" she presses.

"Never!" I scold.

Sara dainties dry with the delicate touch Walt and I have chuckled over since potty-chair days. "Let's read *The Velveteen Rabbit*," she suggests.

"Haven't you got that memorized yet?"

A hard-backed edition, with special inscription, arrived in the mail today: "To Sara. Your favorite book. For my favorite girl." With love from Miss Munro, Sara's second-grade teacher.

I gentle Sara back into the bed. "Remember how you checked that book out of the school library eight weeks straight last year?"

"I was such a funny little girl," she reminisces, easing back onto her pillow.

We share a moment of silence for Sara's stolen childhood.

Cuddled in her new flannel quilt, she closes her eyes and whispers, "Read."

"'There was once a velveteen rabbit, and in the beginning he was really splendid. He was fat and bunchy, as a rabbit should be . . .'"

Steamy tears pinch from Sara's eyes. "It's all so sad," she weeps.

"But Sissy-girl, we're not even to the sad part yet."

"Well, hurry up and get there," she sniffles. "I need to cry."

"Then just cry, Sara."

"I want to cry for myself, Mama. But I feel better if I think I'm crying for the Velveteen. Page seventeen, Mom. Get to page seventeen."

"Real isn't how you are made," said the Skin Horse. "It's a thing that happens to you. When a child loves you for a long, long time, not just to play with, but *really* loves you, then you become Real."

"Does it hurt?" asked the Rabbit.

"Sometimes," said the Skin Horse, for he was always truthful. "When you are Real you don't mind being hurt."

"Does it happen all at once, like being wound up," he asked, "or bit by bit?"

"It doesn't happen all at once," said the Skin Horse. "You become. It takes a long time. That's why it doesn't often happen to people who break easily, or have sharp edges, or who have to be carefully kept. Generally, by the time you are Real, most of your hair has been loved off, and your eyes drop out and you get loose in the joints and very shabby. But these things don't matter at all, because once you are Real you can't be ugly, except to people who don't understand."

"Mama," Sara says, massaging her bare head, "I think I'm becoming Real!"

We laugh and cry and hug. Then suddenly Sara stiffens and huffs over my shoulder, "Quit your spying."

I turn to find Corwin planted in our doorway. Corwin wheels over from C cluster ten times a day to park by Sara's room and stare.

He is black, hip and cheeky. He is fascinated by Sara's cards, toys and bald head.

She is white, protected and refined. She is fascinated by Corwin's clothes, jive and plaited braids.

They trade insults tonight and Sara refuses to play puzzles. Corwin, scorned, delivers a parting zinger, "You can't be no girl. You bald."

"The nerve of some people," Sara fumes. "A boy with braids making fun of a girl with no hair."

Corwin wheelies on down the road and softly the Skin Horse reminds us, "But these things don't matter at all, because once you are Real you can't be ugly, except to people who don't understand."

Dr. Baker gets a cool greeting. "How goes it, Sara?"

"My back is so sore I can hardly walk. That's how goes it."

"Sorry, old girl. You'll loosen up," he assures. "No medicine tomorrow. We're gonna give you a few days to feel better before we begin your second infusion. How about that?"

"Good," she replies. "I've got drawings to finish for that book, you know."

"Right. Why don't you work on them while I talk to your mom."

No dice. She scrunches down under the covers and stares us into the hallway.

"The biopsy didn't show much," Dr. Baker begins. "She's wiped out. Just a few dazed cells swimming around in there. We've got to let her marrow recover a bit before we hit it again. We'll continue the antibiotics and build her up for it."

We look through the glass at the little girl glaring back. She sticks her tongue out and pulls the sheet over her head.

"Sara Beth!" I threaten.

"Spunky little squirt," Dan Baker says. "See you tomorrow, Carol. Hang in there."

When I push through the swinging door, Sara demands,

"What did he tell you?"

"The same thing he told you. They want the cells in your marrow to bounce back before they knock them out again. Your temperature is down, and you should feel pretty good for the next few days. We'll have some fun."

While we plan, I change into shorts and running shoes. "What are you up to?" Sara stiffens.

"I'm going to jog. For thirty minutes."

Walt sneaked my shoes into the suitcase the last trip over. "Keep up your running," he commands.

"I'm too tired and I can't leave her."

"It's good for both of you," he answers. And the B-3 nurses nod their approval.

"Besides," grins Walt, "we're registered for the COH Big Foot 10,000 Meter Fun Run."

And so tonight I will lumber along the nearby Burke–Gilman Trail. Fifteen minutes out. Fifteen minutes back. No more. No less. And Sara will like it or lump it.

"OK," she pouts. "I'll expect you back by seven o'clock." I set my watch and mince purposefully to the elevator.

As I stumble up the access path, blackberry bushes snaggle my legs. I find myself, once again, in the Twilight Zone. What's a country girl like me doing running in the big city? Why aren't I home, gossiping through Dungeness with my jogging partner, Jan? Why aren't we rambling along Riverside, boldly commanding that Doberman to back off?

The Burke–Gilman Trail, arched with evergreens, smells of damp earth, and is nearly deserted this evening. I trot along dutifully, arms low, stride short, breath even. I mumble a few friendly words to passing bicyclists and joggers, but nobody answers.

It's too hard to run without talking. But Jan's not here, so God will have to do. A mile and a half down the path, tired of dominating the conversation, I leave the Lord at the Tradewell, turn back, and concentrate on my body.

My legs are heavy loads, even though I've lost weight. My legs are exhausted even though they've been running thirty miles a week this spring. My legs quiver to a standstill, then limp back to the hospital.

"Ten after seven," Sara reports. "Grandma called. She doesn't approve of your jogging, either."

"At this point," I gasp, "I don't even approve of it myself, Sara. But I'm not going to be humiliated in that race. I'm going to run every night, so you and Grandma better get used to the idea."

Mom is relieved to hear my voice and know that I've not been raped, mugged and maimed. When I joke that it might have been an interesting diversion, she bristles and lands hard. I promise to tell the ward clerk where I'm running and what time I'll return. "Take care of yourself," Mama softens. "A lot of people depend on you."

When I hang up and look at Sara, I crack up laughing. Taped onto the head of her bed is a drawing of a joyous baldie, surrounded by the cosmetic wonders of the world. "Bald Is Beautiful," it proclaims. And the laughing artist posed next to the portrait is living proof.

In the morning, Sara is stiff, sore and bored. But her make-hay-while-the-sun-shines drive stirs, and she asks to "root around in rec-therapy."

"Sorry, Sara," Nancy says. "Counts are in from the lab and yours are low. You can't be with kids in the playroom today. Maybe tomorrow."

"But I need to get busy on a Father's Day present," she argues.

"Maybe tomorrow." And Nancy bustles about her business.

Sara's sadness grabs the physicians on rounds. They cluck around their forlorn little chick, and she peeps forth her problem.

"No biggie," says Patti. "After your bath, you can have a private tour of the playroom, before it officially opens for the day. You'll find something to make the best Father's Day gift ever."

"We'll expect great things happening in here tomorrow, Sara," Dr. Baker warns. Sara doesn't hear. Because Sara doesn't listen. Sara gathers soap, undies, nightie and towel. Sara is masked and halfway to the tub room.

Rec-therapy sprawls ready and waiting. Sara rolls in to clean-papered easels, fluorescent play dough, smiling dolls, unstrung beads and unpotted plants. She is breathless. Dorothy in Oz.

I wheel my little girl and her IV to the piano. She fumbles through her recital songs, "Stars and Stripes Forever," and "Flight of the Swallow," right-handed, then smacks the keys, frustrated. "I won't get to play in the program anyway, will I?"

"Not this time," I answer. "But Mrs. McDaniel said she'd record it for us. Erica and Link will play our part of the quartet."

She doesn't answer, and I escape her sad face by admiring the sewing machine. "Do you sew, Carol?" asks Patti. "You're welcome to use the machine any time." While we discuss fabrics and facings, Sara wanders into the supply room. She snoops into a big garbage can and emerges with a great grin. "May I have a hunk of that clay?" she asks.

"As much as you need," is the answer, and we hustle from our solitary viewing of the playroom with a huge grey glob, a small rolling pin, and some wooden sculpturing tools.

"Dad will go bananas over this," she chortles, plunging one-handed into the mud.

"Maybe you'll have finished the creation when I come back from wig-shopping," I try, expecting the inevitable pout she puts on whenever I announce a departure.

"Could be," she chirps, oozing the clay. "Could be. Remember, just like my old hair. Feathered bangs."

"I'll do my best." I kiss Sara goodbye and float down the hall, buoyed by her good nature.

The chariot awaits. Sue's brown arm hangs out the window of the jazzy forest-green Mercedes SL. Fingers drum the door, bony shoulders groove to the beat, and thonged foot guns the engine. From the tape deck Stevie Wonder croons "Isn't She Lovely?"

"Chic Coiffures express bus," Sue hollers. I roll my eyeballs and fold in to instant culture shock. Sue smells of chlorine and suntan lotion. I smell of bathtub antiseptic and Baby Magic. Sue is shampooed and shiny from curly head to long thin toes. I am greased and grungy from rumpled head to short fat stubbies. Her legs are smoothly shaved. Mine are fuzzy. She says I look "terrif" in my hiking shorts. And since I've always taken Sue's word as gospel, I decide now's no time to change. I smile and say, "Thanks, so do you."

We zigzag to the wig shop, and talk with a middle-aged

blonde bouffant who my, my, mys over Sara's plight, then leans us toward a short brown children's number that can be styled many ways. I offer Sara's head measurements, and she says she'll call when it's ready. "And honey," she rests red daggers on my arm, "I'll throw in some shampoo and conditioner."

We bomb back to COH to fast-talk Sara into the wig we've chosen.

"There is no hair exactly like your old hair, Sissy," I explain. "But you can feather these bangs and the lady says long wigs look really phony."

"We'll give it a try," she concedes.

And I whisper to Sue, "For 129 bucks we'll give it a good try!"

Sara fanfares the uncovering of the definitive Father's Day gifts. "Da doodle de doodle de doot do doo!" Under the damp hospital towel rests an intricately sculptured clown and an etched dish.

"Stunning," I exult.

"I'm going to take my money and buy watermelon candy in the gift shop, put it in the bowl, then when Dad eats it all he'll see the message written on the bottom."

I peek inside and together we laugh at her scrawled "Was it good?"

We plan our trip to the gift shop while I change into my running clothes. My mind is elsewhere.

"Oh, Sissy," I confess, "I'm not ready to run that race on Sunday. Dad is going to know that I've fibbed about how far I've been jogging. And I think I'm in big trouble."

"It never pays to lie," she reminds me. Then with sarcastic sympathy, "You'll make it, Mom. You can do what you have to do."

"Now where have I heard that little pearl before?"

"I wonder," she smirks, and laughs me out the door.

Saturday morning Sara and I make ready for Walt. We hide the clown and dish, change the sheets, spruce the room. And wait.

Weekends snail along on B-3. Rounds are minimal, cafeteria service limited. Our custodian Cora's substitute is sullen, rec-therapy is locked up, and the nurses lack hustle in their bustle. The pace allows too much thinking time. Walt is Saturday's saving grace.

Ooohs and ahhhs announce his arrival. He is jingle bells in June. Walt packs a dozen Sonja roses from our florist, letters and packages from friends and neighbors, the quilt from our bed at home, and smooches for his girls. He is a wind, hurricane force, whipping around our muggy room.

"DeFawn says get Sprite in these roses right away and they'll last longer. Sissy, open this. I'm dying to know what it is. But first, look at this. Can you believe it? A mom of one of my students made it for you. God, I hope he passes his final so I won't have to fail him. Sue T. sent lasagna. It's still in the car. Just heat it a few minutes in the microwave, she says. There's some champagne, too. Sandy sent a couple more scarves. Hey, where's your wig? Put it on while I get the rest of the stuff out of the car. OK?"

When Walt comes up for air, he notices Sara and me blown back onto her pillow. "Boy, are you hyper, Dad," Sara grins.

"Yeah," he sighs, shoulders sagging. "It's that damn ferry schedule."

I slide off the bed. "I'll come with you to unload the car. Sara can open her mail. Be right back, Sissy."

Walt and I stroll the back hallways before we face the June drizzle. He says there is a trust fund for Sara, and it's filling up fast. He says the elementary teachers took up a collection for Sara, and he's got it in his pocket. He says the first grade had a bake sale for Sara, and sold out. He says a whole town's resources are at work for Sara, and he's having a hard time handling it.

We find our favorite place to fold. We sit silent, up against a wall. I blow my nose and make Walt promise he won't think I'm bonkers when I share a feeling that I had this week. He looks skeptical, but condescends to hear me out.

"Well, it was in the night," I begin. "After the biopsy. Sara was asleep and I had that icy grabbed feeling that always comes in the dark. I got up to walk it away, and when I stood by the window looking out at the night, it happened. I had a physical warming and then a feeling of being lightened, like a heavy weight was lifted from me. It was relaxing and peaceful and scary. But most of all, it was for real. I went back to bed and thought about it. Maybe it's like Elmer said. It's God working through all those people. And their energies are channeled into us. And maybe, even though it's hard, we ought to take it and run with it."

Walt doesn't scoff. Walt says he had a similar feeling this week. Walt says he isn't so clear on what it means. But he agrees, no matter what, it will help see us through.

"Let's get the stuff," he whispers. And holding each other

together, we weave up to the parking lot.

Jeannette says if Sara masks and we stay clear of crowds, we can cruise this afternoon. We see every mural in the hospital, check out the snack bar, sit by the big windows and watch the kids from behavioral sciences play basketball. Sara shows Walt the swimming pool, and says she hopes she gets to take a dip this summer. "You will," Walt assures, "you will." And I think Don't make promises you can't keep, Walt.

Jeannette suggests Walt and I go out for dinner. Sara looks stunned and puts on a face. "We've got that lasagna . . ." I begin. But Walt says we'll eat it tomorrow. "I'm not sure it'll keep," I try again.

"I'll put it in the refrigerator with your name on it. Go to Mulligan's," Jeannette suggests. "It's just up in the Village."

"Wipe off that hospital face, Sissy-girl," Walt commands. "You'll be OK for an hour." She cries and I nuzzle her fuzzy head.

"Sara and I are going to try out those new jacks. I used to be a champ," Jeannette brags.

"Beat that sour face off her," Walt jokes, and Sara growls, "No way!"

"We'll be back by seven, Sissy," Walt says, hugging her hard. "Anything sound good to eat?"

"McDonald's fries," she answers.

"Comin' up," her daddy promises.

Mulligan's is just what the nurse ordered. Private, quiet, good drinks, great food. We talk like sixty about Andy and Sara, home and hospital, old friends and new friends, living and dying. Walt says that he never thinks of Sara dying. I say that it is always with me. I share all the details of Lynsey Hunter's transplant and affirm I just know Andy will be a match for Sara. "She is too good to die," I explain.

"I know, I know," Walt grieves. "But what's important now is that this time is good time. We can't think ahead."

"You sound like Dan Baker," I snap. "We've got to direct our energy toward a positive way out of this mess."

"I think positive," Walt growls. "Remember? It's you who thinks about her dying."

I cry, because he's right. The waitress edges over to the heavy scene, and asks if we'd care for another cocktail. "We're ready to order," Walt smiles. That cheesy fakey high-school-annual smile. She writes fast, then scurries away. "She probably thinks you're a sloppy drunk," Walt teases.

"Going through a messy divorce," I add.

We eat, then head home with the fries to find Sara and Jeannette sprawled out, spinning jacks, like ballerinas, atop the Holy Bible. I watch Walt watch our tall, slender, three-to-eleven-shift girl-nurse playing, childlike, with Sara. And I know that he, too, loves my gentle Jeannette.

"Oh," she blushes, "you're back. Well, I hadn't lost my touch, but she beat me anyway."

"Single-handed," Sara jokes. "Get it?"

"Got it," Walt groans. "Here's the French fries."

"I'm really not too hungry, Dad. But I know you can polish them off."

"Right on," sighs Walt. And digs in.

Late at night I lay it on Walt, "Honey, I'm worried about the run tomorrow. I've run quite a bit, but I just feel all wrung out. Would you mind staying with me, just this once. Otherwise, I don't think I'll be able to finish."

"Sure I will," he says. "You'll do just fine. Besides, you've put in more miles than I have these past couple of weeks."

In the dark, Sara clears her throat. Meaningfully. "Good night, Sissy," I threaten.

Sunday morning the sky is falling in. Wind heaves rain against the building, but Walt and I are sunny in our shorts and shirts. Uncle Bill is here to stay with Sara while we're gone. Parents and staff wish us well, and we're off.

The park is jammed with pacers, stretchers, shakers, and my soul mates who warm up by sitting in cars with heaters on full blast.

Walt painfully hunkers in with the women, children and senior citizens lined up behind the nine-minutes-per-mile post. "It's not so bad, Walt. These people chatter, chuckle and really know each other by the end of the race. After all, that's the fun of a run isn't it?"

"You're just not competitive, Carol," he moans. "But by God, you will be today." A quarter-mile up the road the gun sounds and the back of the pack eventually shuffles past the starting line, already three minutes into the race.

The loop crosses Sand Point Way and runs along the Burke–Gilman Trail, then heads over to the Naval Air Station park, down to the water, then back up and home along Sand Point Way. All goes well until the long hill up out of the park. "My wheels are shot," I gasp. "I gotta walk."

"No way," Walt says.

"Go ahead without me," I wail, slowing to a crawl.

"Carol, where is your pride? Look at that sack of cellulite that just passed you. Look at the butt on that broad."

"Well, I'm still ahead of that guy on crutches," I point out.

"Run, you sucker," he threatens. The wind is behind us on Sand Point, and we fall in with some jolly old ladies. They belong to a COH guild, and extol the virtues of the hospital.

I spill our sad story and they mist, hearing about Sara. We all pause passing the hospital to locate our B-3 fans. "There she is!" I yell. "See that spot of red? That's her. And my brother is there next to her. Bill promised they'd be there and there they are." We wave our hearts out and the little group framed in the window waves back.

"Makes it all worthwhile," says the granny on my right.

"A mile to go, girls," barks the coach, and we're off and trotting. The big clock shows sixty-one minutes, thirty-four seconds when we cross the line.

"God," Walt puffs, "if you ever tell anyone our time I'll kill you."

"But weren't those old ladies cute? And those fat ones in their wet T-shirts. I still say the best people-watching is found at the back of the pack, Walt."

"Grab some balloons and let's get outta here."

Back at the hospital we shower and change into our hard-earned T-shirts. Walt tells exaggerated tales of what a baby I was, and Sara loves it. She presents us with trophies fashioned from construction paper.

"Oh, Sissy," I gush, "the best part of the race was when you waved down to us from the window. We all ran a little better after that."

"I never saw you. I never waved."

"Yes you did. I saw your red pj's, Sara. And Uncle Bill beside you."

"It wasn't us," Bill confirms. "We got tired of waiting, so we came back to the room, read books, and made these awards. Honest. It wasn't us."

"God," Walt moans. "We not only made fools of ourselves, we dragged those sweet old ladies down with us."

Ed, the ward clerk, checks in. "How goes it?"

"Great. How'd you run today, Ed?" I ask.

"Well, I made it to church by eleven," he modestly admits.

"Gee, at eleven we were just . . ." The thumb in my back is painful.

"We were just chattering, chuckling and really getting to know each other. After all, that's the fun of a run, isn't it?" Walt smiles. That cheesy fakey high-school-annual smile.

We laze away Sunday afternoon, sharing the newspaper, cherry popsicles and good times with B-3 neighbors.

Walt has fallen head-over-heels for Luis Castilleja, the almost two-year-old black-eyed baby boy in 317. Abel, Luis's father, works in a Yakima alternative school. Teacher talk flows fast and furious. Abel and Walt carpet the third floor with fresh-corrected tests and next week's lesson plans. Kindred spirits.

Luis's mother Jan, balloon-bellied, due any day, waddles my way. I marvel at the thumpy-bumpy egg, ready to hatch, and we labor our previous deliveries. Old wives.

Sara and Danielle, Luis's nine-year-old sister, sidle up shy.

They play separate, but trade smiles now and again. Secret pals.

Dan Baker rains on our parade.

"Hi, guys. Walt, glad I caught ya before you headed home. Could we all talk a bit in Sara's room?"

Dan Baker says we're going to begin the second round of chemotherapy in the morning. Sara cries and carries on. "I've got to finish Dad's present," she sobs. And the bargaining begins again.

"Can you finish the gift tonight?"

"Rec-therapy's closed. No paint."

"First thing in the morning?"

"It may take me all day. Let's go for Tuesday."

"I'll give you until tomorrow afternoon," Dan Baker promises. And when he grabs her toes, she knows the game's over.

"Are they going to start a new IV?" Sara tremors.

"'Fraid so," Dr. Baker apologizes.

"Will you do it?"

"Sure enough," he says, then fades into the sunset.

Sara scrunches under her quilt to prepare for Monday afternoon. Walt's fists rage open-shut, open-shut. And I babble on. "Andy's coming over with Grandma and Grandpa one day this week, Sissy. That's good news, huh?" She huddles harder and doesn't answer.

Walt lies next to the little flanneled lump. "We'll get through this week, Sara. Then school will be out, and when you come home our family can be together all day. You just think on that this week." Walt swallows hard and snuggles his little girl. "Now Sissy, before I go, give me a little hint about my Father's Day present."

"No way, Jose." You just think on that this week," comes muffled from way under the covers. I make Walt promise to call tonight as soon as he gets home. He says that's ridiculous. I say promise, and he does.

On the way back from goodbyes, I see the three weekend admits. The grapevine says they're all transplants. We smile at one another and wave. I love them already.

Sara tidies her bed tray, sets out the clown and bowl, and says that Jeannette has authorized a masked trip to the gift shop in the morning. Quarters and nickels are heaped on the corner of the night stand. "Do you think that's enough?" Sara worries.

"If it's not, I'll bail you out," I assure.

She nests in for the night, then drifts off to dreams of watermelon candy. Sixty cents' worth.

In the morning Sara wears a new silky pink nightie with matching robe. The wig sits jaunty for its virgin voyage, and her money jangles in a rhinestone evening bag. Nancy adjusts the drip on the IV and we're off.

We park the wheelchair. Then Sara, the IV and I fill the tiny gift shop. Sara is Alice in Wonderland. She pets stuffed animals, peeks into paperbacks, touches every trinket, and finally purchases twenty candies. We wheel through rec-therapy for the paint, then set to work. I snap Polaroids (my gift to her father) while Sara strokes finishing touches. Priceless wonders. Labors of love.

When Nancy wheels the prep tray in, Sara begins a low wailing animal whimper. "Knock it off," I command. "Nothing hurts yet."

"But it will, Mama, it will." Dr. Baker whisks in and probes for a vein. Sara's arms are junkie arms. Dan Baker keeps up a steady chitchat, and tells Sara about a teenager who starts his own IV.

"I could probably do that," she declares.

"I'll bet you could," he praises. "You watch so carefully. And you're so brave." Her little noises cease as Dr. Baker pops a vein between the top of her thumb and the top of her wrist.

"Looks OK. Let's have it." Nancy passes the ruby-red Adriamycin. Sara and I clutch hands and close eyes in dreadful anticipation of the nauseous night ahead. As Nancy sets the seven-day Ara-C infusion, Dr. Baker suggests she give Thorazine in an hour or so. Sara objects. "I don't want Thorazine."

"Oh please, Sara," I beg. "It just helps you handle it better."

"I'll handle it myself," she cries. "I hate Thorazine."

"Go ahead and try it without, Sara," Dr. Baker allows.

And I'm ticked off. He isn't going to be here to watch her writhe, listen to her wretch. All night long.

By evening Sara consents to Thorazine. Three hours of unproductive heaving have worn her strong will away. She needs help. When she finally sleeps, Dr. Baker checks in. I am slumped, exhausted, against the wall outside Sara's room. "How could you let her go through that?" I accuse.

"She had to see for herself, Carol. She knows what it's like with and without now. She can make her own decisions on the Thorazine."

"My mind understands that," I answer. "But I can't bear to see her go through all that again."

"I know. I know," he soothes. But he really doesn't know at all.

Sara wakes beaten Tuesday morning. She asks that her door be closed when breakfast trays are up. "It's that stink, you know." I bed-bath her and she wears a hospital gown because she doesn't want to puke on her own. She asks for *The Velveteen Rabbit*, and while I read to the sad little sack, a patchwork mirage peers in our window. I double-take, then say, "Sara, Sara, open your eyes and look out the window."

"Is that J.P. Patches? Hand over my wig." She weaves to a sitting position, gropes for her hair, tries to one-arm it onto her head, fails, then flings it across the room. "He'll have to see the real me," she whispers, and flops back onto her pillow.

J.P. Patches, the television clown, comes on soft and sweet. He leaves his jollies in the hallway, and touches Sara's cheek with his patched white glove. "Sara Kruckeberg. That name sounds familiar to me. Are you a Patches Pal?"

"I watched you every day when I was a kid," she whispers. "And when my brother was three, you wished him, 'Happy Birthday to Andy from Sequim. Look in the dryer.'"

"Ah yes. I remember," he smiles.

"I thought you would," she plays along. "Say hi to Gertrude." And then she sleeps.

I watch J.P. sag slowly off to rec-therapy. Shoulders hunched. Big shoes leaded. And I know I'll never tune in to the J.P. Patches Show without remembering. Clowns cry too.

THREE

Aᴺᴰ what did Dad fix for supper tonight, Big Boy?" I pump. Every night when my boys phone, I ask the same question. And almost every night I get the same answer.

"I think it was chicken."

When Andy turns the receiver over to his dad, I tease, "One of these days you're going to cluck when I answer the phone, Walt. Did you fix a vegetable?"

"Yes I did," he testifies. "Peas. How is she today?"

"About the same. Tired and cranky. Not hungry."

"Did she draw?"

"A little bit. She perked up for the mail. Be sure and thank everyone for being so faithful. It really is the highlight of her day. Does Andy talk about Sara? Does he miss us?"

"He doesn't talk much about anything. He's mad at Grandma because she won't let him rock in her chair."

"I know. She told me he rocks so hard that he either tips over backward or the chair scoots all over the living room. It drives her nuts. She asked if it was OK if he did his therapeutic rocking at home."

"Well, he's doing it now. Can you hear the chair?" Walt holds the phone so I can hear the squeak-squeak-squeak of the old brown Lazy Boy.

"Is he holding his Thumbkey Monkey? Is he snuggled in his red blanket?" I ask.

"Yeah. I'd better get him in the tub before he falls asleep. Let me tell Sissy-girl goodnight."

After their fond farewells, Sara hands the phone back to me, and Walt moans, "Are you letting her talk baby talk? God, she's never done that in her life. Why is she doing it now?"

"I don't even hear it any more," I smile. "I don't know why she does it. Maybe it's being around all these babies." Sara knows what we're discussing and yells, "Wah! Wah! I want my bottle!" I laugh, delighted. It's the only spunk she's shown all day.

But Walt warns, "Tell her to shape up before the weekend or I'll beat her buns."

I repeat his threat to Sara, and she smirks, "Low platelets. I've got low platelets. If he spanks me I might bleed to death."

He hears her and laughs, "Keep her happy until we get there. Tell Jennifer and her mom hi for me. I love you."

"Love you, too. Kiss my boy. Night-night."

Jennifer is our neighbor down the block, room 310. She is three going on thirty. The first time we set eyes on Jennifer, she sashayed up the hall, followed breathlessly by her entourage: a mom, a dad, two teenage sisters, an adolescent brother lugging suitcases, and a banana cart (usually reserved for transporting reclining patients) heaped with a stuffed-animal menagerie and hundreds of dresses.

Jennifer is a movie star, batting her baby-blue eyes and smiling tolerantly at adoring fans. Now she is back "home" at COH, ready for a bone-marrow transplant, the last-ditch effort to rid her elfin body of cancer.

Still new at the game, we marvel that Jennifer and her family play it with such ease and agility. Jennifer passes from sure hand to sure hand, and is never fumbled. On weekends, the whole team lounges in 310. Since Jennifer is in protective isolation, the family masks. Their eyes smile and laugh as they love the goose-downed baby, gussied up in Sunday best. Walt and I take our time and learn a lot on weekends, cruising by Jennifer's room.

Weekdays, Marge the Mama holds down the fort. On good days they do puzzles, read books, dress dolls. On sad days they cuddle on the couch.

I tell Walt about Jennifer's out-of-the-blue announcement, "Well, I don't want to grow as old as my brother Jerry!"

"Why not?" Marge chokes.

"Cavities," she replies. "I don't want cavities. You know I'd have them, the way I love sweets."

Walt cries.

Tonight as Jennifer sleeps, Marge arrives at the communal living room right outside our door, to rest her nose rubbed raw by the mask, to smell something besides her own breath, to grieve and believe with other cancer-cluster parents. Once Sara drifts off, I pad out to join them.

B-3 friendships are hard, fast and immediate. In a crunch, on the brink of losing what we love most, there is no time to tiptoe. Sure-footed we plunge, heart first, friends forever, in five minutes.

Helen, big Greek mama from Washington, D.C., crashes

the party. She heaves to, drops anchor, ties up to the nearest rocking chair, and rests head in hand. Stubby fingers twine black curls, heavy eyelids droop at half mast, and a pillowy bosom rise-falls, rise-falls. Garbed in black polyester and a stretched-to-its-limits T-shirt proclaiming People in Seattle Don't Tan, They Rust, Helen is the oldest sailor on our sea. When she performs her chanty, we tune in.

She tells of Taki's cancer, but says more about his character. Almost four, he's been fighting his A.L.L. for two years, and has been unable to maintain a remission. There are no more drugs for Taki, so he's come to Seattle for a bone-marrow transplant. "Some people think we're fruitcakes dragging him clear out west for something this risky. But he's a helluva fighter. I can't pack it in until he does. Ya know what I mean, kids?" We nod, pretending that we do, but all we really know is that Taki is a chip off the old block.

"He's known nothing but hospitals for two years. How they'll keep him isolated in that room for three weeks. . . . He'll give 'em hell on horseback, friends. He's an animal."

We chuckle, remembering the spent syringes Taki used as one-shot squirt guns this afternoon, drenching unsuspecting aides.

We smirk, remembering Taki on the intercom ordering lobster, artichoke hearts, Top Ramen and a nurse, "just to talk to."

A puffy-eyed, chunky Sunday-go-to-meeting-suited man waves, gives me a shy smile and ducks into 314. "Have they diagnosed his baby boy yet?" I whisper.

Gayle James answers, "A.M.L." Big tears flood big eyes. "Mr. Ayers is a pastor."

"God Almighty," roars Helen. "Good luck, big guy. I've

known a few like him, and sometimes they have a harder time than the rest of us. They think they can pray it away. Well, I gotta head back to the house before it's morning allright-already. See you all tomorrow, kids."

Helen plows out to the house COH has for families of children with cancer. I gather my nightie and towel and head for the showers, the weight of the preacher-man on my shoulders. When I pad back down the hall, Mr. Ayers peeks out. "Can you spare a minute," he smiles. "I need to talk to someone."

"Sure," I answer. "I'll check on Sara and be right over."

Clarence Ayers grips the metal bars of David's crib in one hand and a Bible in the other. "I think they've made a mistake," he begins. "Look at him."

Brown-skinned, plump, soft dark ringlets framing beautiful baby cheeks, eyelashes curling over sleeping lids. He is a cherub. And I am so sad to know him and his doubting daddy.

"He'll be two in September," Mr. Ayers says. "What I think is, he has a virus. Since they gave him the blood and the antibiotics he seems all better. My congregation's been praying nonstop. Look at him again. He looks healed, doesn't he?"

"He is the most beautiful baby I've ever seen," I answer. "But that doesn't mean he can't have cancer. What did the doctors tell you?"

"That the bone marrow says he has A.M.L. They said your daughter has it, too. Did you ever doubt it? Did you make them recheck her?"

"We doubted it. For sure. Because she is too good for it. But in the end, we had to accept and get on with it."

"Well I'm going to make them do the tests again tomorrow before they start treatment. I believe in the power of prayer."

"So do I. And I'm sure they'll do whatever you want done.

But if David needs treatment, hang on to the power of prayer,"
I smile.

And he smiles, too.

We talk about our families. He has a five-year-old son and
a two-week-old baby girl. His wife must be home with the baby,
so Clarence will be the hospital parent. He asks about operating
the microwave in the nutrition center, about the shower room
and the clean sheets, about chemotherapy and hair loss. When I
leave at two in the morning, I know he has accepted and is ready
to get on with it. And I know that I love him.

"God bless you," he whispers.

I want to hug him, but I just say, "Thank you. Sleep
well."

It feels right to be the comforter instead of the comforted.

Helen steamrolls the hallway, gearing down at our door.
Eagerly Sara puts down the paper doll, plumps the pillow,
secures her scarf, flexes her fingers and lies back in anticipation.
The best medicine of the day bellows on in.

With my eyes on Sara I ask, "How's Taki, Helen?"

"Mary, Mother of Jesus!" she wails. "I can't keep under-
shorts on that little poop today. And the nurses are tired of him
flashing his bare butt."

Sara gasps, as I knew she would, as she does every time
Helen opens her mouth. With a wink, not a word, we rejoice
together over this irreverent ball of fire and her equally irreverent little poop.

Sara turns frisky, slides out of bed, and exclaims, "This
I've got to see!" While I gather up the tubing, unplug the pump

and tie on her mask, Sara clucks over Helen's attempts to beautify Taki's behind.

"Sara, Sara, Sara. He's got junior Jockeys with trains, planes and race cars. Red briefs, blue briefs and Superhero shorts. God knows I do my best, Sara. You believe it, don't you, my sweetheart?"

"Absolutely," she replies. Blessed assurance.

Sara scuttles to Taki. The pump, Helen and I scurry to keep up. His face is smushed to the glass, black eyes wistful, waiting for Mom. He spies our parade, makes a goofy face for Sara, which she sends back, then zeroes in on Helen. He demands she return. Now. She fires off some mean Greek, then repeats in English, "I'll come back in there when you pull on some pants." He considers the ultimatum, but is swept away by the captive crowd outside the window. Taki flashes first a grin, and then some skin.

"Jesus wept," moans Helen.

"That child," roars Sara. "I love that child!"

Sara's eyes, above her mask, are dancing, but the band stops playing when Helen says, "Carol, we're going to dinner tonight, late, after the kids are asleep. You're coming with us, sweetie. You need a break."

Sara is wary-eyed, sensing betrayal. And I waver, weighing hospital Hungarian goulash against Seattle seafood. It's no contest. "Nine o'clock, Helen. I'll meet you in front."

Helen enters the bare-butted lion's den and I face the wrath of Sara, who begrudges my evening out. She pouts. She accuses. She sobs. I come on much stronger than I feel, insinuating that she is selfish and spoiled. Filled with the guilt I have laid upon her, Sara accepts.

She chooses my dress, votes for high heels and pantyhose,

and says, "You need a shampoo." By nine, I have the first-date flutters. I kiss Sara goodbye. She pats me, says, "Have fun," and I trip to the elevator, nervous, excited, guilty. And free.

My new friends are waiting. Patti, the cancer-rehabilitation therapist, Denise and Steve, the Canadian parents of year-old David, and Helen, tonight's chauffeur. Since neither Helen nor Denise and Steve are living in the hospital, I assure them that their children are asleep and comfortable. And we are off and running.

Latitude 47 is a classy joint. I worry that I will drop my whole week's allowance here tonight. Our conversation is fast, furious and full of cancer. The diners near us lean in to listen. We are an intriguing group.

"Get this," says Steve. "Five days after David is diagnosed with A.M.L., I call the hospital to tell Denise I've run over Leona, our three-year-old. Her leg is in smithereens. She is in traction for a month at Vancouver General while David's having chemo across town at Lyons Gate."

The diners shy away, horrified, but we close in and laugh big belly laughs. Helen gets control first and blurts, "I go to Congress to get funding for Taki's transplant, bring the family to this soggy city of Seattle, check him into COH, Dr. J. gives him a bone-marrow aspiration and the damned kid is in relapse! So, we have to pull off another remission before they'll touch him. We did it. Kissed his hair goodbye again. But we did it."

We roar, rowdy, boisterous. And the other diners back off, no longer wanting to hear. No longer able to listen.

We are freaks. There is anguish in my laughter. What am I doing here with a one-legged cancer therapist, a couple of Canadians, and a wild woman from Washington, D.C.? Why me? Why us? Why Sara? And I want to go home to B-313 and have my little girl tell me about it one more time: "Why anybody, Mom?"

Helen doesn't waste time on red lights, so I am home in a hurry. It is midnight and COH looms large, a dusky pink sleeping giant. The automatic entrance doors yawn, and I tiptoe in, hoping to sneak into bed without waking Sara. B-3 cluster is dark and quiet, save for one light at the end of the hall. B-313, Sara's room. Two shifts of nurses are nestled together at desk. One of them whispers, "Here she comes."

I panic. Something is wrong. Quickly, Nurse Marshall reassures me. The evening shift joined the night shift to help Sara welcome me home.

They dog my heels and hide behind the door as I enter the room. "You waited up," I chirp.

Back erect, arms folded, brow crinkled, eyes fixed on the wall clock, she demands, "Have you got any idea what time it is? Just where have you been and what have you been up to?"

Snorts and guffaws from outside the room break my dumbfounded silence. The little old lady hears them and calls out, "Tell her I was worried sick." They creep in and report that, indeed, Sara was ready to send out a posse. But, since all is well now, they wish us goodnight and leave. And I know that they know my Sara is something else!

Relieved that I'm safe, she relaxes, leans back and tosses me her scarf. "Well, fix us a cup of tea," she sighs, "and tell me all about it."

On morning rounds, Dr. Baker says he'll mosey by later today when Sara's chemo ends, to talk about *going home*. He is perplexed when we do not trip the light fantastic upon hearing these magic words. But we are no longer babes in the woods. We know home is not the safe, secure haven it used to be.

Gayle James peeks in to chat. They can go home for a weekend pass if Gayle learns to care for Erin's H.A. line. Because baby Erin's veins refuse to be successfully stuck anymore, a Hickman hyper-alimentation line has been surgically threaded through her jugular, exiting out the chest. When not being used for infusion, the plastic tubing must be flushed, then capped with clot-preventing heparin. Gayle is nervous, but trembles off to practice on the bedraggled, yet ever-smiling, H.A. doll.

Sara and I hang out, trying to convince each other we're excited about going home. I am no longer her source of all knowledge, worthy of blind trust. She is afraid to be my full-time daughter. She is stick-legged, raccoon-eyed, a lighter shade than pale. I am afraid to be her full-time mama.

Before dinner, Dan Baker removes the IV, and while Sara rediscovers two-handed, ten-digit living, the doctor lays the familiar ground rules: normal temp and good fluid intake for twenty-four hours and we can, once again, fly the coop. I tell him I'm worried, and he shrugs, "What's the worst that can happen? She gets sick and you have to come back. Maybe that'll happen. But maybe it won't."

I attempt a smile, while he adds that if all goes well, we will return in a week for a bone-marrow aspiration, and hope it shows a first-round remission. If leukemia cells are still present, we will be readmitted for drug "intensification."

"Go for it," he pats, and whisks away.

I call Walt from the pay phone downstairs so Sara won't hear me blubber that I'm scared spitless to come home. Walt says put on the blinders. Concentrate on the bathtub and the new bubbles he'll buy me. He says we'll keep Sara relaxed and happy. He says we'll fatten her up, sit her in the Sequim sunshine, and let her sleep with her big yellow cat. He says she can phone friends, fly on her swing set and play with her brother. And best of all, he says, she can kiss her daddy goodnight—in person. When he pauses to catch a breath, I can't wait to be home. "Gotta pack. Talk to you tomorrow," I laugh. "Buy some wine and change the sheets."

I ride the slow boat to China back to B-3, and deliver Walt's orders to Sara. "Keep cool and drink up. The cat's awaiting at the foot of your bed." She brightens, tosses me the plastic pitcher, and commands, "Fill 'er up!"

Sara follows orders.

Walt and Andy barge into our room, take-charge happy faces intact. I draw back, chip-on-shoulder tired face ready to clash head on. "I've got all our stuff garbage-bagged and loaded onto the cart," I bark. "You can haul it out to the car. Then come back for the suitcases and quilts. I want to be ready when they sign the release forms."

"Relax," soothes Walt. "Andy and I need to stretch our legs a bit."

"Hand over the keys," I snap. "I'll haul it all myself."

"OK." Walt shrugs, refusing to take the bait. I snatch the car keys and stomp my way to the loading zone.

"Are you mad to be coming home, Mama?" Andy worries, tagging along beside the cart. And I'm brought up short.

"Oh no, sweet boy," I sigh, stooping to hold him. His

tight clench and hot tears plead for me to slow down, turn around.

I hear what he's saying.

Dr. Baker is sitting with Walt and Sara when we return. I put my arm around Walt, and he knows I left the bitchy broad downstairs.

"You're all set," Dan Baker announces. "Release signed, local pediatricians notified of your return. See you in a week."

Andy bounces ahead, Walt and I follow arm in arm, and Sara straggles behind, holding up her jeans, chastising Walt for forgetting a belt.

Sara can't go up on the ferry—count's too low—so Andy delivers her heart's desire: a corn dog and root beer. We plan menus all the way home. I whisper to Walt that the dietician told me about a flavorless calorie-supplement powder that I can sneak into Sara's food. Walt grabs his gut, and begs me to keep it out of his sight.

At home, Andy tells Sara the Olts are on vacation and he is feeding their animals. She asks to help, and they troop off, hand in hand. Job completed, homeward bound, Andy yells what he always yells at the corner, "Beat ya home, Sissy!" With reflex action, Sara is off like a racehorse, still clutching her jeans. She pounds into the front door. Victorious. I want to cry, but instead I shout what I always shout, "Use the knob to open that door!"

Grandma bakes macaroni and cheese for our dinner, and Sara scarfs it down. I telephone to tell Mom the good news, and she says buy the magic powder and she'll really load the next recipe.

Walt and I tuck the kids in, then work hard to talk about something other than the spot we're in.

In the midnight blue of our bedroom, we weep. Food is for fat now. Not fun. Talk is in earnest now. Not jest. Sex is for comfort now. Not joy. "Isn't life lovely. Isn't life gay. Isn't life the perfect way to pass the time away?" Bull-honkey! I'll burn that kitchen plaque tomorrow.

After two days at home, Sara winds down like a clock. We take her in for counts, and she is almost too weak to walk. Dr. Turner says to watch her fever, and he will check back with us this afternoon.

We swing into Nickersons' fruit stand on the way home. Sara smiles perky for her special friend, Kelli Nickerson. While Walt and I visit with Dale and Georgia, we decide to take Kelli home with us for a while. "Kelli hasn't got a cold or anything," Georgia frets, "but she looks so grubby. I hope she's OK." I worry a little too, but Georgia will never know it. We must care for Sara's emotional health, I reason, as well as her physical well-being.

Sara is a poor hostess. She lies limp on the couch, dozing in and out, burning hot. Sweet Kelli plays quietly beside Sara, and they share understanding expressions from time to time.

When Dr. Turner calls, he says Sara's counts are very low. I report her temperature is 102°. "I'll call Seattle," he sighs, "and we'll make a decision."

The handwriting's on the wall. I head down the hall to pack bags, Walt takes Kelli home, Andy rocks furious, and Sara pulls a pillow over her head.

The phone shatters the silence. Dr. Turner says Sara must return to COH, but will be loaded with antibiotics first. We must bring her to the emergency room in Port Angeles, where a nurse will administer the injections. We dump Andy and his overnight bag at Grandma's house, and we all cry. Sara tearfully teases her brother, "Why are you bawling? You're not gonna get shot in the butt." He hugs her hard. Her attempt to cheer him, and his attempt to be brave, only make me sadder.

The injections are intramuscular and painful. They bleed freely, so the nurse gauze-packs them before we move on. Sara sleeps all the way to Seattle. Walt and I are silent. We don't have anything to say.

Walt parks in the loading zone so I can get a wheelchair. Sara won't walk. We wait a long time in Admit, and it makes me mad. Sara is immunosuppressed, and here we sit in a waiting room full of people. My mean glares and snorts are futile. It's an hour later when we are finally escorted to B-3.

Jeannette and Sara grab hands in greeting. B-313 is ready and waiting. Dr. Baker is coming up specially to do the admit exam. With this piece of news, Sara rises like Lazarus from the grave, says she will head down to get a popsicle while she waits. And could she please have flowered sheets and an electric bed? She leaves and we laugh. From down the hall we hear Charlie, a retarded leukemic, call, "Sara back? Sara back? Hi, you big turkey."

"You are disgusting," Sara grins. Charlie grins back.

Dr. Baker is on a high. While he fiddles around with Sara, he spies my book, *Passages*, lying on the couch. "I'm through my midlife crisis," he confides. Got a great marriage and I'll be a father this fall. What's this blood all over your butt, Sara? Gonna order you some platelets, girl!"

She pouts and he promises, "We'll infuse them during the night, and you can sleep right through them. I'll personally start the IV, so it'll be a winner."

Jeannette wheels in the prep tray and tells Sara that Dr. Badura's on call tonight for A-3, and if his service is slow, he's planning a sing-along. "He's really good," she blushes, and I cast Walt a knowing glance. I told him I detected furtive tenderness between those two. Walt rolls his eyes at my told-you-so expression.

With the winner IV pumping antibiotics, Sara ponders platelets. "I hear music!" I cheer. "Come on. Let's go." She balks, but Walt hoists her into a wheelchair and we're off.

Only the night lights illuminate our hall as Dr. Badura and Adrian strum lamenting folk tunes. I feel like a Girl Scout again. "All we need is a campfire and a few stars," I whisper to Walt. "Then we could pretend we're up at Camp Kirby, the camp of our dreams, where the ocean just ripples and sparkles and gleams!" Walt groans.

"Pick up the beat. You're puttin' us all to sleep," yells Ed, the evening ward clerk. "How about 'Old McDonald?'"

"Had a turkey! Had a turkey!" roars Charlie.

"That figures," grouses Sara. Everybody laughs.

In the middle of a "gobble gobble here and a gobble gobble there," comes an anguished cry.

"I gotta pee. *Now!*"

Jeannette runs to the four-year-old little man, makes ready to wheel him to the bathroom. But he orders, "Bring the pee pot. I don't want to miss the songs." Our nurse scuttles, but, alas, the fantastic four informs her, without missing a beat, "Too late. I already peed. Eeii-eeii-o."

Dr. Badura's beeper intrudes on our mountain music, and the rest of us trickle off to bed.

We're home again. Close-knit. Family.

"Tonight," I tell Walt, "Camp Kirby's got nothing on B-3."

Sara slumps exhausted into her special-order electric bed, craving sleep. But the night has just begun. A long-haired vampire taps timidly at the door. "Come back in the morning," grumps Sara.

"I need zee blaaad tooonight," spooks the young lab tech. Everyone laughs. Except Sara. She whimpers, but examines her fingers, looking for a likely candidate.

"No fingerstick. Gonna be an arm poke tonight, Sara. Roll up your sleeve."

"I hate arm pokes," she wails. "I'm not going to have any blood left." Walt rubs Sara's bruised legs while I hoist her nightie sleeve. The vampire sucks blood, slaps labels on vials, grabs his tray and clink-clanks into the darkened hallway.

Once more Sara crumples under her quilt. Walt and I change into bed clothes and flick on the eleven o'clock news. Jeannette soft-steps in to whisper goodnight and administer antibiotics and Tylenol, for Sara's 104° fever. The night shift will be in to take cultures and administer platelets, she says. Gentle Jeannette watches Sara sleep, listens to short hot breath, touches fiery cheeks and then mutters, "It'll be a long night, Sara. I'm so sorry." With a sad little farewell nod, Jeannette heads homeward.

"Let's try and catch a few Z's while we can," Walt suggests. We nestle in, drift off to the comforting drone of the pump, then blink wide awake to the glare of the overhead light. Sara sits mean on the edge of the bed, waiting for the night aide to get her to the bathroom.

"We need a clean void specimen, Sara. You want me or Mom to help you?"

"My Mom, of course," growls Sara.

"Well! If you're gonna be that way, maybe I won't party all night with you any more." Sara manages a wispy smile and the snappy little aide giggles. While we collect the specimen, I ask Sara just who this good buddy is, and why I've never met her.

"You're always asleep when she's here. She takes my vital signs in the night. And if I can't go back to sleep, we talk and play games. She has cats, like me, and maybe she's going to bring me some catnip. Her name is Karen."

While we tuck Sara back into bed, I say, "Pleased to meet you, Catnip Karen," and she chuckles a quiet night-shift chuckle. Walt bellies up under the sheet, the great white whale, and groans, "Stop the world, I wanna get off."

Sara confides, "He snores, too."

Kathleen, the night-shift RN, rolls in with a tray. She is older than most B-3 nurses, soft-spoken, all business. She cultures Sara's throat, nose and bottom. Sara is too weak to resist. Silent tears soak the pillow while Catnip Karen promises Sara some hand-me-down Nancy Drew mysteries.

The ward clerk intercoms that the platelets are up, and Karen fetches them while Kathleen changes IV tubing. Karen must check Sara's vital signs every half hour while the platelets infuse. She smiles her apology and promises to tiptoe.

We settle in a third time, and every half hour I am aware of Karen coming in and out of our room. Some time before dawn, Sara moans that she's hot and itchy. Walt and I bolt up to attend her. The bed light shines on Sara's flushed, welty face. Walt wanders into the hallway for help. When Kathleen arrives, Sara thrashes hysterical. "I'll get the Benadryl," Kathleen whispers.

"I hate this. I hate this," Sara wails. And we sit beside her until the antihistimine takes hold and she sleeps that zonked-out drug-induced sleep.

"From now on," Kathleen advises, "we'll just assume she's going to react, and give her the Benadryl when we start the platelets. Then she won't have to go through this every time," Walt and I nod agreement.

But from left field comes a small voice, "No way. I hate to sleep, you know." But sleep she does. Until a morning lab tech arrives for more blood.

Sara lies low for the next few days. The cultures show no bacterial infections. Dr. Baker says Sara suffers from leukopenia, a very low white-cell count resulting in unexplained fever. It is standard procedure to treat these fevers with antibiotics just to make sure all the bases are covered.

As Sara's temperature drops, her spirits rise. She challenges her dad to a domino tournament, craves yogurt and makes new friends on B-3. The toddlers grab Sara's head and heart. She becomes their voice. Mamas ask Sara how the procedures feel, if the chemo affects moods, if food tastes different. Sara is honest and reassuring. But Sara is sad when they leave. "Oh Mama," she sighs. "It's worst for the little ones. They hurt and don't even know why."

"But they handle it, Sissy," says Walt. "God, I love the way Stormy lives up to her name." Stormy's a runny-nosed nineteen-month-old fire-breather. With the face of the grim reaper, she flings baby bottles at offending physicians, pinches lab techs and spits at nurses. It is understood that Stormy is too mean to die.

"And maybe, Sara," I add, "maybe they're young enough that they'll have no memory of the pain they've suffered. I bet you don't remember much of yourself as a two-year-old."

She nods, but isn't convinced. "What about Cassie?" she questions. "What's good about her?" Cassie is a Downs syndrome baby diagnosed with A.M.L. And she breaks Sara's heart. Cassie's body can't tolerate chemotherapy, and though nobody's told us, and we haven't asked, we know Cassie is doomed. She sits in the hall and smiles, waiting for a skinny, run-down mama who visits less and less.

"That's a hard one, Sissy," I mutter.

"Let's cruise," says Walt.

Mom and Dad bring Andy over. He hits the deck, cock of the walk, heads for the popsicles, and looks too big, too broad, too brash to be here. As he bounces off the wall, Walt and I tackle him and haul him away so Grandma and Grandpa can visit with Sara. When he asks to visit "rec-room therinkey," Walt and I share a knowing glance. Andy has a thing for Patty Hingston, the rec therapist. When Patty greets Andy we know the feeling is mutual. She calls him, "my right-hand man," and he stands taller, grows older right before our eyes.

"Will you set up blocks for Ahmad, Andy?" asks Patty. And even though Ahmad frightens Andy, he nods yes. Ahmad lies on a cart, bald, drooly, jerky, and swings a rubber ball hanging from the ceiling at a stack of large cardboard blocks. "Just leave Andy with me and go for a walk," Patty encourages. And we do.

Walt and I hole up in the corner of the cafeteria and discuss Sara's upcoming bone-marrow test. We pray for her remission, but need to know what comes next. "Why won't they talk to us about a transplant? Why won't they even test Andy to see if it's a possibility? Maybe you need to talk to them, Walt.''

We plod back to Andy. He labors, cheeks aflame, sweaty-backed, grinning, ''Great hit.'' He has eyes only for Ahmad. Patty says he has not wavered once from his task. ''He is a super-special five-year-old.''

We study our baby boy, somehow grown older and wiser beneath his heavy load.

My parents and my boys ferry home, leaving Sara and me to our routine. Though we cherish our family togetherness, it exhausts us. Though we feed from the visits of family and friends, we are jealous that they steal time from our cozy two-some.

This morning Sara lets it all hang out, and blurts, ''Some-times I like it better when it's just us.''

''Sara Beth!'' I frown. And she hides her face and cries.

''I love them so much, Mama. And I always want them to come,'' she weeps. ''It's just that it's so noisy when they're here. And you spend all your time going out with Daddy and Andy. And *I'm* supposed to be your job. Remember?''

I settle beside her and tell her I understand. I love them so much too, but it's true, they overwhelm me and divide my loy-alties. ''I'll let you in on a little secret, Sissy,'' I confide. ''I talked about all this with Daddy, and he understands. In fact, he feels the same way when we come home. Dad and Andy have their little set-up too, and we sometimes mess it up.''

''The nerve,'' she grouses.

''But Dad and I decided if we can talk about it and laugh

about it, we'll get through it. And don't feel guilty about your feelings. Dad and Andy are a team. You and I are a team. But when we're together we just have to work a little harder to be a family again."

Sara sniffles and grabs pens and paper to help her mull over our conversation. I give her a hug and answer the ringing telephone.

It's Walt's mom calling from Tacoma. She phones every few days and visits occasionally. She battles Parkinson's disease and the stress of her only granddaughter's illness has taken its toll. Laura's speech is weak and slurred today.

"How's it going?" she asks.

"Pretty good," I answer, more cheery than I feel.

"I've a favor to ask and it's hard for me." A long pause.

"Well, go ahead," I laugh, feeling a little queasy. Walt's mom is into miracles and has hinted that if we just have enough faith, everything will come up roses. Walt bluntly puts down her convictions, and I play the middle man: On the one hand I plead, "If it makes her feel better, don't argue. Let her be."

And on the other hand, I defend, "He believes more deeply than you think he does. Let him be."

But now I sense a choice to make, a side to take.

"I'm going to a healing session this afternoon. Devoted to Sara." Another long pause.

"That's nice," I breathe, waiting for the other shoe to drop.

"We will lay on hands. Since Sara won't be here with us, I'm asking you to lay your hands on her head at two o'clock. That's when the healing will take place. Will you pray with us? Can I count on you?"

If I say no, I'm a heathen. If I say yes, I'm a hypocrite.

Sara always naps in the afternoon. Today I plan to walk to the laundromat and wash clothes while she sleeps.

"Did you hang up?" Laura laughs, nervous.

"No," I answer. "But I have to think it through."

"OK. Just remember two o'clock. I'll talk to you tomorrow. Give Sara my love."

"Love to you, too."

When we hang up, I am very angry. Not with God. God and I have come to terms. I pray for our family's strength to cope. And so far, so good. No, my gripe is not with God.

It's with the fundamentalist pastor and his wife who visit Sara, read religious tracts, and ask often if she's accepted Jesus Christ as her personal Savior. For only then may she enter the Kingdom of Heaven.

It's with prophets of vitamins, carrot juice and laetrile, who prey on our confusion and desperation.

It's with "healing groups" who lay on hands and false hopes. It's with all those people, not caught in our crunch, inflicting their beliefs on us, the Captive Audience. And oh so vulnerable.

I steam from our room and boil over near the nurses' station. Dr. Baker and Dr. Jackson usher me to the nearest corner. I unload my sob story, expecting unqualified sympathy. When I lapse into intermittent sobs, head down, Kleenex twisted, Dan Baker speaks.

"You're probably right, Carol. They have no claims on you and your family. Except maybe one. They love you. And if you can remember that they do it all for love, maybe you can see clear to forgive them for the times they hurt you."

I skulk back to B-313, lie down beside sleeping Sara, and decide I'll leave for the laundromat at 2:05.

I stagger back to B-3, toting a pillowcase packed with clean clothes, armloads of mail, and a Little Kitty inkpad for Sara's Little Kitty rubber stamps.

"Ho-ho-hooold it, Jolly Old St. Nick," calls Dan Baker. "Just looking over Sara's counts. They're comin' up pretty good. Bone-marrow aspiration in a couple of days. OK?"

"Merry Christmas to you, too. Just let us know, so we can get ready."

"Will do," he promises, and noses back into his charts.

Sara fidgets, bright-eyed, waiting on the edge of her bed. I dump the goodies beside her as glad tidings pour from her. Jane Agostine, schoolteacher and friend, called while I was gone. She's coming over tonight armed with home movies of Sara's reading group performing original one-act plays. "And there's sound, too. I told Jane we could use a hospital tape-recorder. Can we go get one? Now?"

"Sure. But don't you want to do mail first?"

Sara dives into it, after carefully laying one letter aside. "I always save Mrs. Marcy for last, you know," she confides.

I nod, remembering.

Geri Marcy phoned shortly after Sara's diagnosis. "You don't know me," she said. "But I wonder if you'd mind if I correspond with Sara. I live alone and I've got the time . . ."

"It would be wonderful. Mail means everything to her."

Geri Marcy writes long, rambling, super letters, filled with raccoons feeding, ships sailing, gardens growing, life living. Sometimes there are trinkets: lace hankies, old jewelry, pressed wildflowers, yellowed poetry. Hand-picked for Sara. Old friends, these pen pals.

Early evening Jane, lugs in with presents, projector and boyfriend Pete. "Popcorn," Sara pipes. "We can't have movies without popcorn. Take some change to the snack bar, Mom, and buy that kind you make in the microwave."

Jane and I follow orders, leaving Pete teaching Sara to juggle apples. We walk slow, talk fast, and cry a little.

"She looks great," Jane says.

"We'll know how great in a couple of days. After the bone-marrow." But put that away. Tonight we sit tall in the saddle. Riding high times.

When we return, the projector is honed in on a cleared wall, Sara sports a new Helen Haller Cougars T-shirt, and Pete looks sheepish as Sara giggles, "We made applesauce while you were gone."

"She's cute, but she can't juggle," shrugs Pete as I scoop smushed apple into the trash can.

The home movies are jerky. The sound out of sync. And Sara loves them. Backward. Forward. Anyward. Over and over again. When classmates wave to her, she waves back.

Jane and Pete leave late. As I tuck Sara in, I ask, "And what was best about today?"

Tucking the film reels under her pillow, she grins, "No contest." Sara sleeps with a smile on her face, but Ralph wipes it off in the morning.

On rounds he tells Sara that he must perform a bone-marrow tomorrow. She tenses, whimpers, then starts to prepare. She draws pictures of it, writes stories of it, talks forever of it. The nurses are fascinated when she hauls out her box of stickers and pastes some on her skinny butt. "A little surprise for Ralphy-boy," she cackles.

Sara skitters all evening, revealing stickered buns to anyone who'll look. Sara chatters all evening, revealing detailed apprehensions to anyone who'll listen. Sara winds down near midnight, leaving me too keyed up to sleep. I amble the dim hall, drink tea at the nurses' station, and read Sara's flow sheet, her hospital report card. Mostly, the nurses chart blood pressure, temperature, heart rate, what goes in and what comes out. But occasionally there's more personal reporting. I love it when the flow sheet says, "good spirits," "happy day," "had fun with brother." Tonight Jeannette pens, "Spent most of shift preparing for a.m. bone-marrow. Ready as she'll ever be."

Which is not very ready at all. Ralph rolls in at eight and says it'll be about an hour. Sara says no way. She wants to wait until her dad gets here. But Ralph won't budge. "See you about nine, Sara. Then you'll have the whole day to goof off." She turns her back on him and slams her head into the pillow.

"I'm going to grab a cup of coffee, Sissy. You watch cartoons and think about how Ralph will laugh when he sees your behind." I kiss her goodbye, but she flinches under the quilt. Nurse Marshall thumbs me out the door, sits down, and rubs sympathy into the bump on the bed.

In the cafeteria I slouch over breakfast and the newspaper. Halfway through the front page, the intercom commands, "Mrs. Kruckeberg, return to B-3. Mrs. Kruckeberg, return to B-3." I bolt from the dining room, sick to my stomach, take the back stairs three at a time, run the hallway, and beg the ward clerk to tell me what's happened. He reads my stark scared face, and apologizes, "Oh, I'm sorry we frightened you. It's just that they're ready for the aspiration. Sara's in the treatment room, but she won't let them do anything unless you're there."

"Well, I should hope not," I flare. "If they told her nine,

then they should wait until nine." Mike shrugs as I huff away.

Sara lies tight on her back, tense and mad, hands gripping the sides of the treatment table. "OK, Sara. Here's Mom. You can roll over now," Ralph soothes.

She spits fire but obeys, shivering hard. "Hey, Sissy," I say, "I'm here now." Then softer, "Wait until Ralph gets a load of your rear-ender."

She allows a tiny upturn of her white lips.

Ralph pulls down her panties and winces as he spies the messages.

FRAGILE. HANDLE WITH PRAYER

TRY A LITTLE KINDNESS.

"Oh Sara, you and your stickers aren't going to make this easy for me, are you?" Ralph preps, then pokes, and misses the mark. Sara wails when he says he has to do it again. I cry with Sissy, but my heart aches for Ralph. Finally finished, we roll an angry little girl from the treatment room.

Ralph apologizes, then sighs, "Please save those stickers for somebody else."

Sara slouches in purse-lipped, pinch-eyed silence. "What're you thinking, Sissy?"

"That is the last bone-marrow Ralph will ever give *me*, she hisses. "He poked me twice and didn't even laugh at the stickers."

"Yeah, I know," I sympathize. "I wonder why that happened?"

"Because he didn't pay good attention and he doesn't have

a sense of humor," she snaps.

"I guess you're right, Sara. It couldn't have anything to do with the fact that he cares about you and was nervous about hurting you. And it doesn't count for anything that he was almost in tears after the aspiration." I exaggerate just a little.

The guilt trip works. She puddles up and concedes the possibility. "I think I'll make a card for Ralph," Sara sniffles, and sets to it while I finish the newspaper.

A piece of me dies when I glance at the entertainment section. Kenny Rogers appears in the Coliseum next week. Last April we promised Sara and Andy that our family would be there. Big summer splurge. But that was a hundred years ago.

I wrinkle Kenny's simpering face, and stomp him into the trash can. Walt's arrival saves Kenny from being kicked clean into the hallway.

The roses are mixed this week, red, pink, yellow and white. There are Polaroids of the new flower shop, and our farmer friend Bob sends photos of two calves for Sara to name. "The brown and white one loves to eat," Bob writes. "The black and white is sweet and shy."

"Ralph and Jackson!" laughs Sara.

"Perfecto!" Walt agrees. "I'll let Bob know."

"Ralph needs a little cheering up, Dad," confides Sara. "He goofed up my bone-marrow and had to poke me twice. He feels terrible."

"How do you feel, Sara?"

"Just weal sad for poor Walph," she worries, in that sicko Shirley Temple voice that drives Walt up the wall.

"Weal sad?" he mimics, and she frowns ferocious, then laughs.

Sara and Walt open presents and mail, play dominoes, and

visit the Red Box. Dr. Baker says he'll have the results of the aspiration in an hour or so.

While Sara naps, Walt and I hurry down Sand Point Way for lunch. I try to tell Walt what it's like to leave the air-conditioned hospital after yet another week of being forever cold, inside and out. What it's like to feel the sun, not just see it. What it's like to see fat kids with hair. What it's like to taste greasy fast foods.

"Welcome back to the real world," grins Walt, pulling into the Burgermaster.

I pick at my salad while Walt scarfs down the Burgermaster combo with shake. "We'd better move on out," I worry. "An hour's almost up."

"I think I'll grab another burger on the way," says Walt.

"Oh, honey, you don't really need that," I sigh, reaching across the table to pinch more than an inch.

"Back off," snaps Walt, smacking my hand away. "I just keep thinking that if I eat more, she'll get better."

We head back with high hopes and no burger.

Dan Baker meets us outside Sara's room. "Let's sit down out here." He motions to the heater vents. We sit down and the cold air blows up my shirt.

I shiver. Walt paces. Dan Baker sweats. "Well, it's still with us," the doctor begins.

"Damn it," slams Walt. "I should've eaten another burger."

"Walt! I can't believe you said that!" I gasp. And we are hyenas.

Dr. Baker is stricken, sure we're finally over the edge, and he rushes to bring us back. "The marrow actually looks pretty good. Close to remission. I'm sure we'll get it with another round. In fact, I'm recommending a shorter drug course this time. Two days Adriamycin, four days Ara-C."

We get control and hear what he has to say. He hesitates and adds, "We're going to want to begin some compatibility studies to check out transplant possibilities. Is Andy around?"

"He's home. But we can have him here any time," I say, a little too fast, a little too loud.

"No grand rush," he assures. "Tell me about the hamburger, Walt."

While Walt shares his compulsions, I break the news to Sara. She wails, but calms when I tell her about the transplant typing. "They must feel sure of a remisssion to go ahead with those tests, Sara."

She nods as Walt and Dr. Baker join us.

"Lookin' good, kiddo," cheers Dan Baker. "We're gonna poke your brother and your mom and dad for a change. OK?"

"Great," she grins.

Dr. Baker explains that there are twenty-five percent odds for a sibling match, and a five percent chance for parent compatibility. He warns, once more, that these are not good odds, and that a transplant isn't a sure-fire miracle cure. "We'll discuss it further when we see if it's even a possibility," he adds.

When we're alone, Walt says he's going after Andy tomorrow. The hematologists want to take blood samples while Sara's counts are up, before beginning her third round of chemotherapy.

Jeannette comes in for vital signs, then says, casually, "Got new orders, Sara. Let me see your IV arm." Sara warily gives it over as Jeannette unwraps an alcohol wipe.

"Are you going to remove it?" yelps Sara.

"Those're my orders," shrugs our nurse.

Sara takes an hour-long, two-armed soak, to scrub the moldy stink from her IV hand. Sara plants flowers and paints pictures in rec-therapy. Sara croons to beautiful Keeta, a Cambodian refugee made vacant by spinal meningitis. Sara clucks over A-3 babies, buys barrettes in the gift shop for the wig she never wears. Sara snags a wheelchair and lets fly down the fifth-floor ramp.

Sara, once more, makes hay while the sun shines.

Walt returns with our son on Tuesday for the 9 a.m. blood draws. Andy shadowboxes B-3's corridors, and Walt dubs him our "great white hope."

"Gimme the poke, gimme the poke," Andy bounces, his dukes up.

"You just wait," Sara warns. "It hurts."

"Nuh, unh. Cause I'm tough. Not a sissy."

"We'll see," Sara says, flopping back with a wicked smile. Lab techs and Dan Baker clatter in. "Who's first?" he blasts.

"Dad!" blurts Andy, snuggling into the blankets with his sister. Sara laughs big, hugging her boy, while Walt puts out his arm. Then it's my turn. And finally Andy shoulders to the front line.

His plump tanned arm never wavers as blood fills vial after vial. I close my eyes and pray that his red stuff is the right stuff.

"Hey, you OK, big guy?" Dan Baker asks. Andy nods, but his lips are chalk, his forehead clammy. "All done now. Lie down there with Sara. We'll get you some juice."

The macho-man stretches out with his sister and mutters,

"I didn't feel a thing. Do you really cry when they poke you, Sissy?"

"Sometimes." He rolls his eyes and sighs disbelief.

"Well, you'd cry too if they stuck you every day, Andy," she spitfires.

"Nuh unh," he answers. And she doesn't argue because she knows he speaks the truth.

Dan Baker says it will be a week or ten days before the typing is completed. If Andy and Sara have inherited identically, Sara will be a candidate for a bone-marrow transplant from her brother.

While the kids pitch in to one good playtime before Sara's third round of chemo begins, Walt and I ramble around the neighborhood. Four transplants are currently isolated on the floor, and we yearn to join their ranks. Their fifty-fifty survival rate rings in like the new year, since our current odds are zilch.

Late in the afternoon our boys head for the ferry dock. Sara promises to send Andy a letter on her "Don't let the turkeys get you down," stationery, and he says he'll send photos of our pets. Walt gives me my "allowance" and makes his standard dumb comment, "Don't spend it all in one place." And I make my standard dumb reply, "Get outta here!" And they're gone again.

Just as Sara and I begin a game of Uno, Dan Baker lopes in with a tall thin palomino pony of a girl. Long straight hair, bangs that brush the tops of horn-rimmed glasses framing eager-to-please eyes. Laurie Fouser, our new intern. "Nice to meet you, Sara," she says, then lets fly a wide-open, you've-got-to-grin-back grin. And we're hooked.

"My doctor at home is a girl doctor," Sara announces.

"Wendy Mouradian diagnosed her," Dan Baker says, then booms, "Well, Sara old girl, Dr. Fouser is going to start your new IV. The medicine is ready and waiting."

While Sara protests that she is *not* ready and waiting, Jeannette wheels in with the cart. Dr. Fouser takes Sara's long puny arms and begins the increasingly difficult search for a decent vein. She settles on one near the top of the wrist, and as she prepares to go for it, I notice our jolly intern's hands are blue-tinged and trembly. The chosen vein's a bummer, Sara whimpers, and Laurie Fouser probes again. This time she hits pay dirt, and Jeannette hands over the ruby-red Adriamycin. As the medicine injects, Dr. Fouser's face is pink-splotched concentration. She exhales only when the syringe is empty.

"Ya done fine," I praise, feeling like her mother. I love that she cares enough to chill, quiver and blotch breathless. I love that she says, "Yeah. I did." I love that she whinnies up a belly laugh, then snorts it in again.

Sara's eyes dance around Dan Baker. "Girl doctors are great," she teases.

"Oh yeah? Just remember, I taught her everything she knows."

Sara's ready to prowl. When we return from our usual haunts, Sue, Carrie and Little Karen, an A-3 aide who lives with Sue, are waiting at our door.

"I'll order the root beer!" Sara shouts.

"And I brought the wine," Sue whispers.

Let the wild rumpus begin.

Sara and Carrie turn up the radio and rock the night away, while Sue and I sip wine from paper cups.

"I don't think I'll be sick from that Adriamycin this time," Sara laughs. "I feel great!" She plops on the bed and twirls her wig high in the air around her big toe.

When our cups are empty, Sue packs up her gang and splits to make the drive-in movie. Sara sad-eyes their departure, but thanks them for the fun evening. "Next time bring Cheetos," she grins.

Sara lies stone still and quiet while I scoop out the room. "Did all that action poop you out, Sissy?"

She stares at the bathroom doorknob and nods a tiny nod.

"Do you feel a little queasy, Sissy?"

She stares at the doorknob and nods again.

I settle her under her quilt, turn off the overhead light, and tiptoe to my bed while she continues to zero in on the doorknob.

And then, "*Surprise!* We decided to bag the movie and come back to the party! Cheetos Cheetos everywhere!" And Sue tosses bags of chips onto Sara's bed.

"Get those things outta here," Sara bawls. And retches into the blue bowl.

Sue backs into the hallway while I collect the Cheetos. Then we hug goodbye, laughing, crying, the corn curls crunching between us, while five-year-old Carrie sorts it all out. "It'll be better tomorrow," she promises. And I believe it.

Jeannette is with Sara, dickering over the Thorazine dose. "OK. We'll go with a half. Be right back."

"Sit with me, Mama, while it goes in," Sara asks between heaves, and I smile yes, screaming inside at the absolute rotten unfairness of this whole mess.

Sara thrashes, moans, finally crashes as the drug takes hold. Jeannette smooths the few wisps on Sara's head, bustles into the bathroom, fusses with the potty pans, scrubs her hands, touches my slumped shoulder, and apologizes, "I'm so sorry."

"Well, it's not your fault," I answer. "But whose fault is it, Jeannette? That's what I'd like to know."

"That's what we'd all like to know. I'll check back in a few minutes." And she slips into the bright lights of the corridor.

Soon after, I trail her with my nightgown, towel and soap. The shower room is locked, so I sit at the tea-party table to wait my turn. Aching for someone to talk my troubles to. Nurse Karen kneels beside me and says, "How goes it?" I take one look at her young, delicate, tender concerned face and blubber my brains out.

"You know what she asked me today?" I sob. "She asked me to save that little red velvet coat with the white fur trim. And you know why? So *her* little girl can wear it. And you know what? She may not live to ever have a little girl."

"I know. I know." Karen cries.

"And Andy. What about Andy? Nobody understands about Andy. They love each other more than anything. How will I ever explain it to him if she dies? Walt can't think about her dying. But I can't not think about it."

"I know. I know." Karen pulls Kleenex after Kleenex from the little box. Compulsive. "And you need to think about it because it's a real possibility. But then you need to put it away and do what you're doing so well. Live each day." She grabs my hands and adds, "Don't give up on that little red coat."

"Never," I smile.

Marge emerges from the shower room and plops wordless beside us. Adrian clogs past, double-takes, then hums the "It's a Bad Night on B-3 Blues."

Sara wakes groggy in the morning, but with a new set to her jaw. I ask if she wants breakfast and she ignores me. I ask if she wants to watch TV and she ignores me. I ask if she's ready for a bath and she ignores me.

"Darn it, Sara. I know you feel crummy, but you can still be reasonably polite and answer me." And she ignores me. "Sara!" I shake her foot.

"What, Mama?"

"Answer me when I talk to you," I scold.

"Oh, I'm sorry, Mama. I didn't hear you. I was busy thinking away the sickness."

"You were what?"

"Thinking away the sickness."

"How do you do that?"

"I don't know, Mama. But I have to concentrate. Why don't you go have breakfast?"

"I will, Sissy." And when I kiss her she smiles a tolerant, been-there-and-back smile that makes me proud. But sad.

Dr. Fouser sits at the nurses' station. When she asks about Sara, I report that she's busy thinking away her sickness. The nurses glance up and Laurie Fouser nods, "Good for her."

Sara's next days are silent, hard-working days. She refuses food and Thorazine, vomits just once or twice. The staff is interested in her new powers, but she can't or won't explain them. I would rather watch her sleep, drugged and peaceful, than watch her concentrate, tranced and distant. When I share my feelings with Nancy, Sara eavesdrops, then gently chastizes, "But it's really not your choice, is it, Mama?"

Sara's third course of chemotherapy ends. I strip the room and Walt shuttles us home. We keep visitors away this time, hoping to ward off the phantom fevers. But by the third day, Sara's counts have bottomed, her temperature's up, and the COH hematologists say she must be re-admitted for antibiotics.

"We could hospitalize her here," Dr. Turner, our pediatrician, phones. "It's up to you." Walt, Sara and I confer quickly and agree to give it a go. Walt could spend more time with Sara. I could spend more time with Andy. We could all spend more time together.

By late afternoon Sara sits perky in an isolation room at Olympic Memorial Hospital. The room is cramped and unfamiliar, the nurses older and strange.

"A special nurse will be up to start your IV in a few minutes, Sara," a motherly sort advises.

"At my hospital doctors do the IVs," Sara announces.

"Well, this nurse is specially good with kid veins."

"We'll see about that. This kid hasn't got many veins left, ya know," Sara brags.

The white cap gives me a she's-a-mouthy-twerp-isn't-she look, and I offer a weak shrug.

"Well, well, well," says the IV nurse, drying her hands with a paper towel. "I've got my goody tray here. Let's go a-hunting for a big fat vein."

"Left arm. I need my right one," brazens Sara.

"If that's possible, OK. Let's have it." The left arm juts forth while Sara rests her head on her right hand, fingers drumming. While the nurse massages, prods, searches, Sara rolls her eyes, sighs big bored sighs, and suggests, "Try the top of the hand. There's usually a good one there." The nurse ignores the free advice.

I catch Sara's eye as it rolls my way and give her a that-will-do frown. She twists her mouth to one side and dimples a sassy smirk.

"OK, Sara. I'm going to give it a go." The nurse lays out her tray.

"Is that a plastic needle?" Sara questions.

"Mm, hmm," comes the preoccupied reply.

"Well, I prefer stainless steel, if you don't mind."

The nurse and Sara lock eyes, chest up, and sparks fly.

"I use plastic on children's veins," Nurse stiffens.

"I come from a children's hospital. They use steel. You'd think they'd know. . . "

"Plastic holds the vein open better. Then the IV lasts longer."

"One time Dr. Baker gave me a record-breaking IV—ten days. Steel needle."

"OK, dear," sweet-talks Nurse. "I'm going to give you a little shot of local anesthetic before I start the IV. Then you won't feel a thing."

"Not necessary," enunciates Sara. "They never do that at my hospital."

Nurse bristles. "These plastic needles tend to drag when they go into the vein."

"Just another reason why I prefer a stainless steel. Why don't you go get one. I'll wait right here." Sara retracts her arm. Nurse wrestles it back.

"Two pokes instead of one," Sara mutters. "Reee-dicu-lous."

The plastic needle jabs, back and forth, up and down, wiggle and waggle. Then finally, red blood backs up into the tubing. Nurse tapes it securely.

"Got an armboard?" Sara fires. "At my hospital we use armboards. Immobilizes the arm. IV lasts longer."

"Don't need them with these plastic needles, Sara. Have a pleasant evening, honey. I hope this one's a record-breaker, too." She smiles a tight forced smile, and closes the door firmly behind her.

"Boy, I'll bet she thinks you are a bossy little brat," I unload.

Sara looks stunned at my indignation. But self-satisfied.

"And wipe that little smirk off your face. You were rude. And if I hadn't been so flabbergasted I would've paddled your fanny right in front of her."

"Even with my low platelets?" Sara feigns shock.

I try not to laugh, and mutter lamely, "Well, just don't let it happen again."

"Right on, Big Mama," she jives, and I kiss her when I should clobber her.

There are no sleeping lounges available, and the floor nurse suggests I go home to bed. "Oh no," I gasp. "I always stay with her. I'll sleep in the chair."

"We have children much younger than Sara who survive the night without their mothers. I really think it would be best . . ."

"I'm sorry. It's just how we do it," I assert. "May I have a blanket?"

She returns pushing a wheelchair with leg holders extended, sheets, pillows, and a blanket. We stuff the pillows into the space between the seat and the leg lifts, lay the sheet on top, and it doesn't look half bad. "Thanks so much," I say. "I really appreciate it." Her smile, tinged with pity, implies that though she still thinks I'm a mother hen, she understands our extenuating circumstances.

I shower in our private bathroom, help Sara to the toilet one last time, and crawl onto my makeshift bed.

"How is it, Mama?" Sara whispers.

"Not bad, Sissy," I answer, turning to face her. Then, boom! The bottom falls out, and my butt hits the deck.

"Poor Mama!" Sara giggles, out of control, as I repack the pillows.

Funny the first time, but by the sixth crash I throw it in and watch the grey sky lighten.

In the middle of the morning, I ask for Sara's counts so that I can record them in my book. "Oh, we can't give out that information," answers the lab tech. "Hospital policy."

"Well, I'm sure it's OK," I smile. "I keep track. See, it's here in my *Parents' Handbook*."

"I'm sorry. Not without doctor's orders."

Am I ticked! I call Walt to spout off. "I'll be right in," he soothes.

We go to the A&W for a teenburger. I rattle on, telling Walt about the IV.

"You let her get away with that?"

"Yeah, and I was proud of her!"

About the cozy bed . . .

"Six times?"

"At least."

About the blood counts . . .

"We'll just talk to Dr. Turner."

"I want to go home to Seattle."

Walt is quiet. Maybe a little hurt. But he agrees. "You're right. It's better that way. Today I felt bad leaving Andy at grandma's, but we can't expect him to sit in that dinky hospital room all day. We've established a routine and this is ripping it all apart. You tell Dr. Turner.''

''I kinda thought you'd do that,'' I hedge.

''Coward,'' Walt answers.

''Just explain to him that it's not this staff or anything. It's just different than we're used to.''

''Will do, chicken.''

Dr. Turner sees all, hears all, understands completely. He visits our room. ''It's a children's hospital, and we're blessed to have it so near,'' he agrees. ''I've called over and they're ready and waiting. We want to run some antibiotics before you go. Plan on about four this afternoon.''

Sara promises to be good while I go home to pack our bags. At four-thirty we greet the IV nurse. She removes the tubing, leaving the plastic needle in place. ''Maybe they can just hook you right up again without starting a new one,'' she suggests.

''Maybe. But at my hospital we prefer stainless steel, you know.''

''Right. Keep me posted, Sara. Be well.'' They lock eyes, chest up and nod their goodbyes.

It's evening before we're admitted to B-315, the only un-occupied house on the block. Cassie's old room. The Downs syndrome child with A.M.L. Sara turns frantic, won't sit on the bed or talk to the nurses. She breathes huge gulps of air, holds, then exhales slowly.

''What is it, Sissy?'' Walt kneels beside her.

She scrapes away on the hard, blue plastic chair, turning

her back to her daddy.

"I'll be right back," I mutter. A little frantic myself. I grab Nurse Karen and demand, "Just where is little Cassie? Why isn't she in 315 where we left her?"

"Because she died yesterday, Carol."

"Well, I don't like that," I wail, like a spoiled baby.

I return to Sara, who snorts like a raging bull when I pull her onto my lap. Walt looks helpless, shakes his head, shrugs his shoulders. "It's Cassie isn't it, Sara?" I ask.

"She's in intensive care?" Sara begs.

"No. She died."

The breathing gets harder, faster. Angrier.

As I hold Sara, we see Cassie smile at the balloon Andy ties to her wheelchair. We see Cassie turn yellow as her liver shuts down. We see her surrounded by oxygen tanks and bleeping monitors. We see her draped on the shoulders of our nurses, who take time to rock her.

Finally, Sara cries pinched, broken little tears of resignation. "It's just no fair," she weeps over and over again.

"Excuse me." Jeannette peeks into the room. "Would you mind if we moved you back to your old room, Sara? We'd like to have the little guy who's in there now closer to the nurses' station. Besides, you and your mom just sort of belong down there anyway. OK?"

Sara nods hard. "You need to keep a good eye on those babies."

I go with Jeannette and fall all over myself thanking her. "I'm just so sorry we didn't think about it before you guys arrived," Jeannette apologizes. "It's been a zoo up here tonight."

"Hey, Jeannette?" Sara slides into a wheelchair. "Can I wait in the living room and may I have an electric bed?"

"We'll put Adrian on it, Sara."

"I suppose you want yogurt too. *Yuk!*" Adrian sneaks up behind Sara and tips her backward, leaving her resting on the floor, staring at the ceiling, legs flailing.

"You'll pay for this," Sara steams, as Walt puts the chair back onto its wheels.

While Adrian and Jeannette ready the room, I ask Sara if she wants to talk about Cassie.

"Wait until they see this plastic needle," she clucks. "Wait until they hear there was *coffee* on my meal trays. Let me tell about your bed, Mom. Let me tell everything."

While the intern on call gives the admit exam, noting bruises and bleeding gums, Sara details her Port Angeles overnighter. A little old lady returned from the outback. Sparing no details, adding a few. The audience oohs, ahhs, eggs her on.

It's almost eleven before Sara is tucked in, a new IV (stainless-steel needle) pumping more antibiotics. Blood tests show she is in danger of spontaneous bleeding because of a low platelet count, so Sara must be transfused in the night.

While Walt and Sara sleep, I shower and talk with Nurse Karen about Cassie. Karen says she died comfortable, sedated. Just slipped away. We talk of Cassie's mother, who only visited occasionally, and then for just a few minutes each time. Karen explains that some people begin the grieving process before the actual loss. And maybe, because of Cassie's retardation, the detachment had begun even before the cancer diagnosis. "Don't judge her harshly," Karen gently cautions. "It's different for everybody."

"Right," I nod, remembering the stringy-haired yellow little ragamuffin wrapped like a Rhesus monkey around the gaunt, used-up too-young mama.

Kathleen, our night nurse, sets up the platelets while I edge under the quilt, elbowing Walt to his own side of the bed. "Sleep," she says. "I'll take good care of Sara."

Around two, Sara whispers that she needs to use the bathroom. I bump the pole across the metal door stripping. Sara says wait outside. She'll call if she needs me. I sag on the edge of my bed, waiting. There is a gasp, then a thud. I muscle open the bathroom door, and Sara lies heaped between the toilet and the wall. The IV pole tilts cockeyed against the door frame, and the pump whistles a warning.

"Help, Walt!" I shout, and he lurches from deep sleep, grabs the pole while I lift Sara. We heft her onto the bed as Kathleen comes running.

"She fainted, I think. And fell off the toilet."

"Right," agrees Kathleen. "Her red-cell count is way down. She needs blood, but we thought she'd better get the platelets first."

Sara comes to, says her head hurts. Kathleen turns on the overhead light to check it out. There is a scrape on the side of Sara's head, but no sign of hemorrhaging. Kathleen washes the wound, dabs on some ointment, and says, "Go back to sleep, Sara. It'll be better in the morning." Sara snuggles down and drifts away.

"Call me if she needs to get up again." Kathleen tiptoes to the door. "And try to get some rest."

Sara follows her usual pattern: tired, listless, fever with no specific infection. Walt follows his usual pattern: back to the home front and his boy.

This evening Sara's temperature is lower and she perks along. The Nickersons visit, and when Georgia and I head to the nutrition room for popsicles, Dr. Baker, phone in hand, motions me to the nurses' station. "I'm getting the results of the studies. I'll meet you in the conference room."

Georgia gives me a hug, and says she'll sit with Sara. "Take your time."

Dr. Baker hurries in and shuts the door. I try to read his face, but I can't. "Well," he says, studying a little scrap of paper, "Andy's no match for Sara." I am so cold. Again. Freezing, shaking, teeth-chattering cold. "Can I get you a sweater?" Dan Baker asks, still heaped, perspiring, over the little scrap of paper.

"No, no. Just tell me. Now what?"

"Remember? She'll go on a randomized protocol, and we'll hope for more good days than bad, Carol. I warned you that a transplant was an unlikely possibility. And I'll tell you something else. Maybe this is for the best. Even with a perfect match, kids don't just breeze through a transplant. It means more strong chemicals, massive radiation, and big risks. Maybe a viral pneumonia that we can't treat. Maybe graft-versus-host disease where the flesh peels away, leaving the body open to infection. Maybe intestinal G.V.H., where the gut just rots away. A transplant's not all it's cracked up to be. I'm not sure I'd put my kid through it. Maybe this is for the best. You don't have to make a decision. It's all made for you."

I lay my head on the table and cry for a long time. Finally, "I'd better call Walt. He asks every night."

"The studies are kind of interesting, Carol. Do you want to look at this paper?" I wipe the tears off my face and try to unclog my nose. "See. Andy and Sara aren't even close, but Sara and Walt are almost a match, and you and Andy are a match. Very unusual."

"Yeah," I say, skimming over the scratchy little letters and numbers. "Kind of interesting. Well, I'd better call Walt."

"Hang in there."

"Right."

I use the pay phone near the snack bar, and when I say hi, then start blubbering, Walt knows it's bad news. "Well, shit. We should've expected it, I guess," he says. "One chance in four."

"But I felt so sure . . ."

"Carol, in a way this is easier. We have no choices." And then Walt cries, and I cry, while the long-distance minutes wash away.

"Well, I'd better go back. She'll wonder where I am. I can't tell her tonight. I can't tell her at all."

"Don't. Just wait," says Walt. "We'll do it together. Give her a kiss for me."

"And Andy a kiss for me."

I wash my face with cold water in the public rest room, and trek back to B-3. Dale is reading to Sara, and Georgia waits in the living room. I tell her everything and we cry all over again. "Well," she whimpers, "maybe it's better this way. No decision to make. You can just make the best of every day." Poor Georgia looks stricken when I laugh, out of control.

"That must be the right thing to say, Georgia. Everybody else said it!" It feels good to laugh again. In a few minutes I tell Georgia and Dale to hit the road or they'll miss the ferry. Sara says, "Thanks for coming. Next time bring Kelli." And they're off.

We settle in for the night.

"Georgia has a sweet little pansy-flower face," Sara whispers, just before I fall asleep. "Jeannette is a lily. Taki is a dandelion, bright but kind of wild."

"You are a nut!" I exclaim.

"I am a rose," she giggles. "Gorgeous, but fragile."

"Dad's a carnation. Sturdy and curly," I play.

"Andy's a weed!" she roars. "And you are a skunk cabbage!"

Morning blood work shows Sara's counts on the rise. Her temperature's 101° and she chooses a happy-faced puppy sticker from Ralph at rounds.

Dr. Baker hangs back as the others file out. "Carol, it appears I was a little hasty in my evaluation of the transplant studies. Dr. Johnson looked them over this morning and says the match between Walt and Sara is OK. Of course, there'll be more tests, but the bottom line is the transplant is a good possibility."

"How can it change overnight?" My heart beats like sixty. "You've got to show me so I can tell Walt."

"It didn't change overnight," he laughs. "Come on and I'll explain." We sit on the floor outside Sara's room, and he draws on a paper towel:

WALT	CAROL
A-1 A-27 B-8 B-8	A-1 A-25 B-8 B-36
SARA	ANDY
A-1 A-1 B-8 B-8	A-1 A-25 B-8 B-36

Dan Baker explains, "There are hundreds of genetic markers to inherit. These A's and B's represent some we're interested in for a bone-marrow transplant. What's unusual is that out of hundreds of markers, you and Walt share two in common. Andy got an A-1 from Walt, A-25 from you, B-8 from Walt, B-36 from you, and winds up your match. Sara got an A-1 from each of you, and a B-8 from each of you. Now I was misled by Walt's A-27 into thinking this was close, but a mismatch. Len Johnson says technically it is a mismatch, but since Sara has no markers different from Walt's, the match is OK. *Voilà!*"

"I've got to call Walt."

"Hang on a minute. When you phone, tell him we need both him and Andy back for more family studies. And Dr. Johnson wants to talk to both of you before you decide if you want to go through with a transplant. Listen to everything he has to say."

"Right. May I borrow that paper towel? Thank you. Thank you very much."

I hover a moment outside 313, peeking through the glass. Sara strings tiny beads onto spider-web threads. Delicate, pink-cheeked, perfectly still. She is a rose.

FOUR

SARA continues beading while I telephone Walt, but her ears zap in on our conversation. I read from the paper towel as if it were the Holy Grail. Walt copies the letters and numbers onto the telephone pad at home. He is amazed, pleased and a little bit proud to be the possible donor, and says, "Five percent chance for a parent-child match. God, this must mean something."

"It's a sign, Walt. Things are going our way."

When I hang up, Sara, still zeroed in on her beads, asks, "If I have a transplant, will you live in here with me for three whole weeks of isolation?"

"Where else would I live?"

"I love you, Mom."

I am antsy, leafing through the newspaper. And there's Kenny Rogers again and it is this very weekend he sings in Seattle. I want to do something about it. Need to do something about it. "I'm going for a cup of coffee, Sara. Be right back."

I ease my dollars into the change machine and scoop out a

handful of change. Settling down with my favorite pay phone, I fly into action.

"Concerts West," chirps the receiver.

"Yes. I've a question I hope you can answer. We are unable to attend the Kenny Rogers concert this weekend, and I was wondering if I could get a recording of the performance for my daughter."

"Oh, I'm sorry. I can't authorize anything like that. That's up to the recording artist."

"Well, you see, early this spring we promised Sara she could attend the concert, but then she got cancer. And now we're in Children's Orthopedic Hospital here in Seattle . . ."

"That's awful! Listen. Why don't I give you Kenny's L.A. phone number. Under the circumstances, I'm sure it'd be OK. Got a pencil?"

Got a pencil, but my hand is so shaky I can hardly write. "Go ahead."

She fires off the area code and phone number. "Good luck to Sara," she says. And we've made a new friend.

I pace and sweat a little before dialing Kenny, practicing my lines, feeling guilty using Sara's illness to advantage. But not too guilty.

The L.A. phone rings, just like any old phone. Then a voice, a woman's voice, "Yes?"

"Hello. I'm calling from Seattle . . ." And she's in for my whole spiel.

"Oh boy," she worries. "It's federal law that these concerts can't be taped. Kenny himself couldn't give you permission. You know, pirating and all that. Hang on a sec. I want to check out something."

While I wait, I wipe at the red splotches on my neck and

take my pulse.

"Hi again. I was just checking Kenny's schedule in Seattle, to see if he'd have time to stop by for a visit. But it's really tight. I can't promise anything."

"It's really nice of you to try," I say, thinking, my God, I need a new dress, just in case.

"May I have Sara's address, so that Kenny can drop her a note when he's back in L.A.?"

I stammer through it and she says, "Best of luck to your family."

"Thank you. Thanks a lot."

I float back to B-3 and whip open my address book to K— for Kenny. The nurses can hardly believe I have his number. "Actually, it's just his agent," I modestly reply.

"Hey, let's give it to Social Relations and see what they can do with it," rec-room Patty suggests.

The rest of the week is taken up with thoughts of Kenny. Nurses wonder whether to try to work Sunday, just in case. Mothers drop by to look in my address book, and Sara draws a marvelous portrait of "The Gambler," while the tape plays full blast, over and over again.

Walt and Andy are over on Sunday. The whole floor knows Kenny's not coming—Social Relations got the same "tight schedule" reply I got—but the whole floor waits anyway. Especially Sara, in a long dress and her wig, and me, in my best underwear under my best jeans and shirt, and Helen, with a fresh curl in her hair. And Walt, snickering at all of us.

After dinner, as I send my boys to Walt's folks for the night, I laugh it all off and say, "Well, I really didn't expect him to show up anyway." Carol the Cool.

The Big Greek Mama sputters up and snarls, "See if I buy

any more of his goddamn albums. I may break the ones I've already got!'' Helen the Honest.

When I return to Sara, the wig hangs on the bedpost. "Not even Kenny is worth this," she moans, scratching away at her shiny bald head.

Nurse Marshall flops laughing on the bed and sums it up best of all. "Oh well. All the excitement sure made the week fly by. Right?"

In the morning, Walt and Andy return for more blood work. We arrange for an afternoon meeting with Len Johnson, the transplant hematologist, and my stomach starts to churn. While Sara and Andy watch TV, I unleash all the transplant horror stories on Walt. "Maybe this isn't best, Walt. What if she dies from it and we've robbed her of even a day of her life?"

"Let's save all this for Dr. Johnson, Carol. Let's just forget it until then."

"I don't understand you. How can you forget it until then? This is the biggest decision we'll ever have to make."

Walt rests his head in his hands and warns, "Back off. Will you just back off."

Len Johnson is mid-thirtyish, with parted dark hair and koala-bear eyes. A jowly gentle Australian with a captivating accent. "Have a seat, Mr. and Mrs. Kruckeberg. Walt and Carol," he urges. "Do you mind if Dr. Hoshi sits in on our conference? He's hoping to take the transplant procedure back to Japan." Dr. Hoshi is a short, chipmunk-cheeked man who doesn't speak much English. He smiles and nods, smiles and nods. I like him a lot.

Dr. Johnson goes over our match, pronounces it a good one and presents some history of bone-marrow transplants. They were first done in the 1950s, prior to H.L.A. typing. The results were disastrous and transplants were curtailed until the '70s when H.L.A. typing was discovered. "With the ability to match these particular antigens, we are now able to come up with a fifty-fifty survival rate for transplant patients. A transplant would considerably boost Sara's current odds, which are ninety-five percent chance of irreversible relapse within a year."

"I wish we could just wait and see if she's one of the five percent," I whisper.

"Unfortunately, that's not an option," Len Johnson sympathizes. "The transplant must be done in remission so that there are no cancer cells for the graft to resist. In fact, the best results have been with A.M.L. patients because, by necessity, they are transplanted in initial remission. With A.L.L., a transplant isn't even considered until after two relapses, and then the odds for success are slimmer.

"What kind of statistics do you have on parent-child transplants?" I ask.

"None that are significant, because so few have ever been done."

"I could find them for you, but they aren't valid because of the small sample."

"Did any of them work?" Walt asks bluntly.

"Yes," Dr. Johnson replies. "Your match is technically as good as a sibling match. Although it seems that the younger the donor, the better the success rate. And we don't know why. We have some answers, but not nearly enough. As I see it, the bottom line is that a transplant increases Sara's chance for a normal productive life."

"But I've heard that death from graft versus host is unbearable." I quiver.

"G.V.H. can be horrible," agrees Dr. Johnson. "But death from A.M.L. is no picnic. Look, without a transplant, Sara's next year will be made up of more hospital time for drug infusion, more hospital time for those undiagnosed fevers due to low white count. And maybe one good week out of four where she could go to school and feel reasonably normal. Is that quality living for a child like Sara?" he asks. "Sitting around waiting for the bomb to go off? If the transplant goes well, no more drugs, no more aspirations or spinal taps, no more hospital. Home free."

"If Sara were yours . . ." I ask.

"There'd be no question. I'd do it in a minute."

"I've got no question either," says Walt.

"Include Sara in the decision," Len Johnson advises. "We always do that with teenagers. And from what I hear about Sara," he grins, "she's capable of thinking it through."

"And liable to get huffy if she isn't consulted," I laugh.

"Let me know," Len Johnson smiles, squeezing our hands. From his corner, Dr. Hoshi grins and nods, grins and nods. And we're on our way.

We lay it on Sara as best we can. "Ninety-five out of a hundred children relapse within a year from A.M.L., and don't get another remission." Her eyes widen. "Fifty children out of a hundred survive a bone-marrow transplant and appear to be cured of A.M.L. But fifty children out of a hundred die from complications, or suffer a relapse after a transplant. What are your feelings, Sara?"

She studies the ties on her quilt. "I don't see that there's much of a decision to make," she shrugs, punching the play button on the cassette recorder.

> You never count your money
> When you're sittin' at the table,
> There'll be time enough for countin'
> When the dealin's done.

"That's more than a card game he's singing about, you know," Sara lectures.

"Right," I answer.

"That's my new theme song," she giggles. "Get it?"

"Got it," says Walt. And the gambler bounces to the beat on her hospital bed.

Sara's appetite, cheeks and blood counts blossom. Free to be, Sara marches everywhere, pushing her own IV pole. I trot breathless behind. "Wee Sara Kruckeberg runs through the town. Upstairs and downstairs in her nightgown."

"Oh Mother," she cringes, "don't be so gross." She chums with the nurses, and they treat her as one of their own. Nancy brims with wedding plans and Sara is her best audience. Sara cherishes our invitation, and special-orders stained-glass lovebirds from Touch of Glass in Sequim. When Sara calls home, Walt says, "What's going on over there? You're supposed to be sick, not on vacation!"

"I think it's remission," Sara giggles. "And speaking of vacation, Dad, I promised everyone I'd bring them a surprise from Disneyland. OK?"

"Great," Walt laughs. "Let me talk to Mom."

Sara hands over the phone and sashays into the hall. "I can't believe her, Walt. She is skinny and bald and everybody's darling. She's hyped and hardly ever sleeps. Almost like she's making up for lost time. They're doing an aspiration tomorrow, and if all is well, the IV comes out and we can go home."

"Call as soon as you know," Walt says.

"For sure," I promise.

Sara perches on the vinyl couch near the nurses' station, bright eyes blinking, head tilted, the better to hear, chirping in her two cents' worth. "Come on Sissy, let's hit the machines. I'll buy you a treat." I roll my eyes and shrug an apology for this pesky little person, but Nurse Marshall says, "Hurry back, Sara. So we can see what you buy."

When Sara finally winds down and sleeps deep, I'm glad we decided not to mention the aspiration until morning.

Nancy springs it on her after bath time, during bed change. "Wear those red pj's, Sara. Dr. Pendergrass just loves them and I think he's doing your bone-marrow this morning."

Sara stops mid-panty-pull-up and wails. Nancy snaps in the hospital corners and talks louder. "Final fitting on my gown today. I'm as skinny as I'm gonna be, I guess." Sara shuts up, but gives Nancy a hateful, I'm-on-to-your-diversion-tactics stare. Our nurse squats beside Sara and says, "We'll get it over with fast, Sara. And maybe your IV can come out this afternoon and you can draw me a picture for my new house." Sara softens and one-arms Nancy around the neck. Sisters.

Dr. Pendergrass chatters during the procedure, telling us about the time he himself had an aspiration. He was so tense it couldn't be done the first time and he had to come back the next day. As he finishes the story, Sara whimpers, moans, and the aspiration's over.

And I know that next time I'll ask for this expert.

After lunch, Len Johnson comes in grinning and pulls up a

chair. "Well," he begins, "Sara's marrow is clear, with no abnormal blasts. We've got a remission."

"I could've told you that," Sara smarties.

"I'll bet you could've," Dr. Johnson smiles. "Now, tell me your plans, Carol."

"We'd like to spend a few days at home," I say, "then go to Disneyland for four nights and five days."

"Perfect, just perfect. Build the old girl up a bit with home cooking, then go to Disneyland and forget all about this place. Ride the Matterhorn for me, Sara. I'll stop in to tell you goodbye tomorrow."

I follow Len Johnson out the door—I'd follow him anywhere—and he nods and winks. "She looks supah, just supah. Call Walt and tell him to pick you up tomorrow."

We are joyous as Jeannette removes the IV. Sara scrubs her hands over and over again. Lovingly rubs them together. She dries them, lotions them, displays them on the bed tray.

Purple dots welt where spikes pierced flesh. Three white quarter-moons brand her fingernails, marking three chemical infusions. Dingy tape wraps the green birthstone ring so that it will stay on Sara's chicken-bone finger. Pale, scarred, crucified hands.

"Here, Mama," Sara offers. "You wear my ring until I grow into it again. The tape makes it ugly."

"You hardly notice the tape," I argue.

"I want you to have it." And she folds it into my hand.

"Come to dinner with me, Sissy."

"Do you think I can? Really?"

"Let's ask."

Jeannette thinks it's a fine idea. Sara wears a long print dress, pink tasseled footies, and a pink scarf for her first visit to the cafeteria. We hold hands, but she's two steps ahead of me all the way. Sara treads sacred ground, wide-eyes forbidden fruit, and chooses pizza, green beans, yogurt and chocolate milk. We scoot into my usual spot and she says it's nice to know where I go when I leave her. She eats almost everything, and pronounces the pizza "the best ever."

"It's the same stuff you gag over when it's on your tray," I scoff.

"No way. This is much cheesier."

And I laugh. Because she is so beautiful and funny and glad to be alive.

Sara scurries all evening, dogging nurses, overworking the ice machine, reading riddles to Adrian. By eleven o'clock shift change, her energy level has done me in.

"Let's hit it, Sissy," I plead.

"Go ahead, Mom. I need to wait up for Catnip Karen. She's bringing me a surprise."

"That reminds me!" shouts Adrian. "This jumped into my basket while I was grocery shopping. And it had your name on it." Out of his tunic pocket, the crazy aide plucks New Jello Yogurt Pudding mix. And sure enough, it has her name on it. "To Sara. From Adrian. *Yuk!*"

"Oh thank you," Sara laughs. "I'll bring you a special treat from Disneyland."

"Have fun, Sara. See you when you get back." And he plants a big noisy smooch on top of her head. She grabs him, kisses his cheek, and Adrian faints onto the floor. "She loves me!" he swoons. "I can hardly believe it!"

"Get outta here," Sara flushes. And Adrian exits on hands and knees.

Sara does mouth care, snuggles into her quilt with Nancy

Drew, and promises lights out at midnight. I fold into the hide-a-bed and only half hear what was good about today before I doze and dream that all hell breaks loose.

In the morning I know it was no dream. The 6:30 lab tech trips over empty root beer cans and popcorn tins. Sara, in full makeup, sprawls on her bed that somehow skittered four feet across the room during the night. The crimson-lipped hussy lifts one blue-shadowed eye and growls, "Come back in the morning," then snores through the fingerstick.

"Must've been some party," snickers the lab tech.

"I wouldn't know. I wasn't invited," I yawn.

"There's a note taped on Sara's bed. Do you want it?" As the vampire labels the vials, I read:

Dear Carol,

Sincere apologies for keeping Sara up all night, but it wasn't all my fault. She promised to sleep after helping with 3 a.m. meds, so when we finished, I said, "I'll tuck you in," and she said, "You'll have to catch me first." I chased her down the hall and she took a dive from the doorway and that's when her bed crashed into your bed and you sat up and said, "Be careful. Low platelets," and that made Sara laugh so hard no way could she sleep. Forgive me, but spank Sara. Have fun in Disneyland.

Catnip Karen

"What stinks in here?" gripes Nancy while she takes Sara's vital signs.

"Catnip," drowses Sara. "Fresh catnip."

"Karen brought some for our cats," I explain.

"From what I heard during report this morning, it sounds like Sara ate catnip last night."

Sara chuckles into her pillow, and I tell her to be up and at 'em when I return from breakfast. Ready to roll when Dad and Andy arrive.

We're spilled into the hallway when our boys stroll onto the floor. Dr. Johnson gives final instructions. Relax. Have fun. Forget COH. . . . And call as soon as we're back from California.

He stands back as we love our good Greek neighbors goodbye. If all goes well, Taki and Helen will be home in Washington, D.C. when we arrive back in Seattle for our transplant.

"I'm sorry we met under these circumstances sweetheart." Helen crushes me to her breast. "But by God, I'm not sorry we met."

"I love you, Helen. And that boy is a one-of-a-kinder."

"Carol, Carol, Carol. Take care and call me when you get back here. We'll keep in touch, my friend."

"Forever," I nod.

We celebrate on the ferryboat, and make plans to visit the travel agent.

Sara spends her first days at home getting used to being well again. Those old fightin' words, "Clean your room, make your bed, eat your peas," are back in my vocabulary, and it hits Sara like a cuff on the chops.

"You were a lot nicer at the hospital," she grouses. And I grab her and smooch her and smack her on the fanny.

Sara visits her ninety-year-old piano teacher, Gertrude McDaniel, and they talk wigs. "My hair is so thin," Mrs. McD. confides, "that my daughter-in-law thinks I need a wig. But I don't know, Sara. Tell me how you like yours."

"Well, it's hot and itchy and really doesn't look like my old hair." For emphasis, Sara scratches her head and the wig scoots from side to side. It comes to rest, slightly askew, just like Gertie's little smile.

"Just as I thought, Sara. Just as I thought. Thank you for being so honest."

Sara plays with friends, and Walt takes snapshots of the doll hospital Kelli and Sara create. Baby doll Hanna lies hooked to a sandwich-bag IV, on a Tinkertoy pole. Plastic straw tubing and tongue depressor armboard complete the picture. "You were supposed to forget all this, Sara!" Walt moans.

"Play therapy, Dad. It's good for me."

We decline the annual Independence Day picnic at the Barkers' cabin, and enjoy a family Fourth of July at home. We shake our heads and cluck our tongues at the little girl who braved big needles and conquered chemotherapy—but is afraid of firecrackers.

Sara's best friend, Jill, turns nine on July 6, and Sara is reluctant to accept the party invitation. "You've never missed Jilly's birthday," I encourage. "And your friends will be so glad to see you."

"But Mark and Ryan will be there," she worries. "And what if my wig falls off?"

"They might get an eyeful," I concede. "But they like you for more than your hair. Right?"

She dresses in short yellow overalls, chooses a scarf instead of the wig. I drop her off, and watch as she timidly joins the kids on the deck. They greet her like one of the guys, and she smiles and tightens the knot in her scarf. Jill's mom says stay for cake, but I've got to get away fast. I bawl all the way home.

Cash ("Buy something special at Disneyland, Sara."), tickets ("We had a few left from our vacation. Hope you can use them, Sara."), and best wishes warm our mailbox every day.

Then finally, on July 9, we fly out of SeaTac Airport. Lifted by love.

Sara and Andy nose up to the little windows, and marvel at the earth below. "I am a bird!" Andy bursts.

I smile my nonchalant, world-wise smile, and clue the attendant, "It's their first flight."

"Really," she answers.

"It's Mom's first too," Sara pipes. "And she's almost thirty-four. And it's Dad's second, but his first on a jet."

"Really." She cocks a plucked eyebrow. "Welcome to the friendly skies." And she pins United wings on the kids' jackets.

We snap pictures of the airplane wing, Andy eating dessert, then Sara focuses on Crater Lake. Lunch is hardly digested when the pilot announces our approach to L.A. International.

As we debark, the stewardess invites us into the cockpit. The tan, balding captain asks Sara and Andy to join him at the controls, but they hang back. Sara mumbles, "No thank you."

The stewardess smiles, "Have a wonderful vacation." Then she grabs my elbow. "And good luck to your family."

I look her in the eye, and know that she knows. It makes me angry, this lack of privacy. Not content to merely destroy the innermost, the very marrow, this cancer must announce the affliction to the whole world. Fight back, it warns, and say hello to needle tracks and wasted flesh. Then kiss your hair goodbye.

Walt and I park on our suitcases, and await a Trailways to the Hyatt Anaheim. Sara and Andy whirl around concrete posts, hopscotch sidewalk cracks and get on our nerves. "And to think," I mutter to Walt, "I thought she'd need a wheelchair."

The Hyatt Anaheim is a dream come true. Skylighted tree-filled lobby, a small shopping mall, giant-size swimming pool, and "we have a pop machine right outside our room," gasps Andy.

"Who cares about Disneyland," I tease. "Let's just hang out here and save a few bucks."

"Well, I'm going to Disneyland in ten minutes," Walt announces. "Anyone who wants to can come with me."

It's a short hike to the park, and we decide to go for it rather than wait for the shuttle van. We pay our admission, get our hands stamped, and sail on in to Fantasyland. The souvenir shops hook us right away, and Andy wants his Mickey Mouse ears *right now*. The Mad Hatter is packed with people. While we wait to have Andy's name embroidered on his purchase, Sara draws a deep breath, slides off her scarf, and begins trying on hats, evil-eyeing curious onlookers. She chooses a sun-visored number, and we're ready to ride.

The Matterhorn looms first on the list, and we join a long line. Sara watches the bobsleds screech down the mountainside and anounces no way is she going to climb aboard. "Sure you are," Walt jollies. "Mom'll be right with you. This is fun." Sara sits on the hot cement and says she'll wait for us right here.

"Get up, Sara Beth," I smile through clenched teeth. "I'm a little nervous too, but we're all going to ride. This is fun." She gets up and puckers up all at the same time.

"Sissy's a sissy," Andy taunts, and she hauls off and slugs him. "Didn't even hurt," he toughs. So she hits him again.

"Knock that off," Walt says. "This is our vacation and we're having fun."

"We came to Disneyland to ride the rides. Not sit and look at them. We're having fun," I chip in.

"I wanna look in the shops," Sara wails.

"Later. Not now. We're having fun on the Matterhorn and that's that," I conclude.

Walt and Andy board first, Sara and I climb into the next sled. "This isn't so bad," she says, clenching the bar. "We're having fun."

"Yeah," I agree, gripping Sara's waist. "See, I told you so."

We climb slow and steep, coming nose to nose with icicles, avalanches and the Abominable Snowman. Then it occurs to me. What goes up, must come down. And I remember that I hate roller coasters. We emerge from the inside of the mountain, poise at the peak, and stare at the Magic Kingdom splayed below. Vrooom! Tear, jerk, jolt. We careen the corners of the Matterhorn. Sara screams all the way down. I close my eyes and envision the headlines: "SEQUIM TOURISTS ARE DISNEYLAND FATALITIES."

Icy water splashes away the nightmare as we hit the glacial pool marking the end of our ride. Walt and Andy stand waiting, grinning like fools. "Let's do it again!" Andy cheers, but Sara groans that she can't.

"You big baby," Andy jeers.

"Uh-uh," she flares, lifting up her shirt. "I'm injured." Red marks streak her belly.

"Did you hit the bar, Sara?" Walt queries.

"No, Mom did it," she tattles. "I kept screaming for her to let go, but she just pinched harder."

They all glare their accusing smart-alec glares, and I glare back. "Come on. We're holding up traffic," I command, and the kids race ahead.

Walt plumps my fanny and leers, "Little bit scared, huh?

Don't forget, this is our vacation and we're having fun."

"Keep your hands to yourself," I snarl. "And don't expect me to get on that thing again." Walt grabs the strings of my halter top and says, "At least we know why Sissy's a sissy." And we laugh and smooch in the middle of Main Street.

We stroll through the park, then eat dinner at an outdoor café. Sara's favorite land is Fantasyland, while Andy's ready for Tomorrowland. We decide to take a spin through both, then head back to Main Street for the evening parade and fireworks.

When we hop aboard our boat for a sail through Small World, Walt studies Sara and whispers, "We'll never get her outta here." Her eyes, illuminated by pastel lighting, devour the singing, dancing dolls of foreign lands.

When we float back to the big world, heralded by a big sign, You're Never Far From the Bank of America, Sara dazzles, "I've got to see that again!"

"Bor-ing," replies Andy. "No action, man. A bunch of dumb dolls. Bor-ing."

"Maybe you and I can do it again tomorrow, Sara, while Andy and Daddy do something else," I offer.

The line for Space Mountain, Andy's choice, is miles long, so we settle for Mr. Toad's Wild Ride before staking a spot on Main Street. Bands, floats, Disney characters, all decked in lights in sync with electronic music, dance by while we clap and cheer this whole magic escape.

We sore-foot home, our path lit by galaxies of fireworks. "I can't believe we're here," limps Sara.

"Carry me," begs her brother.

The next two days are crammed with Disneyland, Mexican restaurants, hot sun and swimming pools. Sara sports a super-thin latex racer's swimming cap. She responds to curious glances with an important snap of the cap, stands thin and tall, the epitome of high fashion.

I worry about her scarves and the Anaheim wind, but on the second day, at the entrance to the Magic Kingdom, Sara lays my fears to rest. A gust swipes the blue scarf, and scurries it over the asphalt. Walt and I stand stricken as Sara gives chase, whirling past stunned onlookers, and snatches her kerchief. "Gotta bolt this baby on better," she announces to no one and everyone. And we laugh, her family, the tourists, and Sara Beth too.

Tired of "I want this" and "buy me that," we give the kids their souvenir money and they have at it. Sara spends it all in one place, all on one thing: a magnificent Snow White doll with velvet cape, nylon stockings and silk underwear. Andy ignores his sister's quality versus quantity dissertation, and buys a million cheap trinkets. We choose twenty Mickey Mouse badges for the B-3 staff to wear on their tunics, and one Goofy badge for Adrian. Dr. Balis, Sara's new transplant fellow, gets an extra large Mickey Mouse T-shirt, Dr. Baker gets an infant size for his expected fall arrival. And most special of all, Nurse Nancy rates a blue wedding garter from a saloon in Frontierland.

Sara trembles over even the mildest rides, gripping our hands, hiding her head. When Andy teases her, we take him aside and explain that maybe Sissy needs to save her courage for those big things she *has* to be brave for, and that we must try to understand.

We wait in a long hot line for the Big Thunder Mountain

Railroad ride, weaving in and out of the turnstiles, finally close enough to see the cars rip-roaring up and down Big Thunder. Sara puts on the brakes. "Let me outta here!" And she ducks in and out of the metal railings, a mouse in a maze.

"I'll go after her, Walt. You and Andy ride." When I catch up to Sara, she is crying.

"I'm sorry, Mama, but I just can't take it. You go ahead. I'll sit right here and wait. I promise."

"Are you kidding? I hate those roller coaster rides. No way was I gonna get on that thing. What a relief! You gave me the perfect excuse to back out. Let's get some juice."

She stares at me, grabs my hand, and says, "Are you kidding me, Mama?"

"No way, Sissy. From now on we'll ride only what we want to ride. And if we want to spend the rest of the day on Small World, we will. A deal?"

"I love you, Mom. Especially your chicken parts."

On our last balmy day in make-believe land, we plan to close down Knott's Berry Farm. We are Dad and Mom, Sister and Brother, spit-and-polished. The average American family.

Maybe a little above average.

As we await the Anaheim Fun Bus, we stand sturdy, tanned and well dressed. The pictures of health on that sunny sidewalk. I can't take my eyes off Sara.

She wears the blue plaid sundress Grandma Mary made her, with a coordinating pale blue scarf, pale blue pom-pom socks and pale blue tennis shoes. The muscle tone has returned to her lanky brown hairless legs. Her body, though slender, is cuddly again. And her birthstone ring fits without tape.

A pair of halter-topped bottle-blondes jiggle past the bus stop. Andy whistles, spins his eyes, and squeaks his Donald Duck cap. Sara smacks her palm over his puckered lips, knees his behind, then laughs loud, thrilled by his audacity.

The Fun Bus fumes to a halt and the kids crash aboard to avoid my lecture on unbecoming public displays.

Walt draws Andy as his seatmate, and within seconds, the little boy nods off, sunburned cheeks aflame, drooly mouth agape. "Don't catch flies," smiles Sara, smoothing his sweaty head.

She plays with my fingers. And then, from left field, "How many days will we have at home before the transplant?"

The magic carpet swoops in for a landing, ending our pie-in-the-sky joy ride. We've not talked cancer or transplant for four days. The single reminder of our two-and-a-half-month ordeal is Sara's baldness. We are proud that we have truly lived one day at a time. Made each one count. But now I'm edgy. Sara is rocking the boat.

"How should I know?" I bristle. "I'm to call Dr. Johnson as soon as we get home. Will you go on the log ride with me, Sissy?"

"I love Dr. J.," dreams Sara. "I'm excited to give everyone the Disneyland presents. Wait until Nancy sees my Snow White doll."

And I know the jig's up. We have not conquered Sara's cancer. We have chosen to gamble. Sara is beginning to prepare herself, and the rest of us, for the final roll of the dice.

Knott's Berry Farm is long lines, dusty roads, Frontierland. Aboard a rickety ore car, we rumble round a coal mine; snuggled into a log, we whoosh a waterfall; and with aching arms, we pan for gold.

But thoughts of the future tarnish the shiny yellow metal. Our family is tired and tense as we crush to the back of the next-to-last Fun Bus.

Sara scrunches beside a friendly-faced young woman. Andy nudges next to Sara, and is held in place by Walt, standing in the aisle. I stumble behind Walt as the bus grinds into gear, shuttles weary tourists to Hotel Row.

"I don't see why I couldn't," whines a lumpy man in a seat near me.

"I told you, you could," groans the woman beside him.

"You said we'd miss the bus," he says.

"We could be takin' the next one," she says.

"Well, I didn't want to go on Montezuma's Revenge alone anyway. Traipse a few thousand miles to find out you're lily-livered. And I'm not riding one of these goddamn Fun Buses clear out to Universal Studios tomorrow either."

"It's a Trailways—air-conditioned," she says.

"I don't believe it," he answers.

"Believe it," I butt in, squinting at the dough boy. "We took that tour yesterday."

"Don't miss it," adds Walt. "It's great."

Jelly Belly and Pitiful Pearl are from Montana. The kids stayed home with Grandma, because it just didn't seem fair for them to see Disneyland during childhood, when Mom and Big Daddy had to wait until they were grown-ups. I fight the urge to puke on their polyester pants suits.

At each hotel stop, the crowd thins out. Walt and I carry sleeping Andy to an empty seat in the middle of the bus. Sara chatters with her seat partner, who she has discovered is an Australian exchange student.

We hear Sara chuckle, "Bet you're wondering why I'm wearing this scarf on such a hot night. Chemotherapy. That's why." A hush swishes through the half-empty bus. Even the Odd Couple stop their yammering.

"Bald, except for a few strands," she crows, aware of her captive audience. And to her parents' horror and grief, then pride and joy, she spills her guts.

Sara spares nary a poke nor a puke, recounting the past months in a jolly-good voice. As passengers disembark, they use the rear exit to glimpse this teller of tall tales.

As she details the transplant procedure, I am impressed with her total grasp of its implications, and her eagerness to get on with it.

"Hyatt Anaheim," announces the bus driver. We stagger to the door and wait for Sara. "Have a good trip home, Jenny. Nice meeting you."

"Good luck, Sara. Be well," whispers Jenny as the door hisses shut.

"She was nice," smiles Sara. "I'm glad I knew her."

"I'm sure she feels the same," I answer.

.   The plane slides in on a drizzly SeaTac runway. Goose-fleshed in Southern California attire, we stash sacks and suitcases into the Oldsmobile, and head for the ferry dock.

We know we're really back when Sara shouts, "Look! It's Dr. Wendy!" There, loaded next to us on the boat, is our doctor-girl. "Get her shirt out, Dad, so I can give it to her now."

Dr. Mouradian is thrilled with her gift, and whips it on right over her dress. Sara and Andy deliver a nonstop travelogue and Wendy hangs on every word.

"Remember, I'll keep my ear on you. My spies are every-where," Wendy hugs us as the ferry docks.

Finally home, we spread our treasures all over the couch, eyeing, touching, trying, and it's midnight before we tucker out. "I've got to call Dr. J. in the morning, Walt," I whisper.

"Well, it's not morning yet," says Walt.

"She's sixty-three pounds, tanned and terrific," I report to Len Johnson.

"Supah," he laughs. "Best news I've heard all day. Carol, we need to talk over a couple of things. I'm sure you're aware that Sara's good veins are few and far between."

"Right," I agree.

"Well, I'd like Dr. Hickman to put in an H.A. line before the transplant, if it's OK with Sara."

"She's right here. I'll ask her."

"Yippee! No more pokes!" whoops Sara, loud enough for Dr. J. to hear. "A line. Just what I was hoping for."

"Good for Sara," Len Johnson chuckles.

"When do you want us back?" I ask, thinking a week, maybe two.

"I'll meet you in clinic tomorrow afternoon. We'll have the admit ready."

We emerge from the inside of the mountain, poise at the peak, and stare at the Magic Kingdom splayed below.

Sara, Walt and I don matching Mickey Mouse shirts for our trip to Seattle. Long-lipped Andy wears his to Grandma's house. In the car Sara chatters and sorts gifts, anxious to see her friends, detail her vacation and get on with it.

The Mickey Mouse Club wows B-3. They admire Sara's tan, the meat on her bones and the sparkle in her eyes. Nurse Nancy mutters, "She's all well."

"Seems all well," Walt corrects. Nancy nods, hugs herself, then bustles about her business.

The kerchiefed good fairy flits around the ward, bestowing gifts on the chosen ones. Dr. Balis snags her into 313 for an admit exam. He wrestles his souvenir T-shirt over his X-tra Tall Man coat and tie, proclaims it a perfect fit, and says he can't wait to show it to his two-year-old son.

A soft-spoken whooping crane, Frank Balis accomplishes twice as much in half the time. When Sara talks, Frank Balis listens—with a captivated side-smile. He is a people-oriented researcher. A rare bird.

"You're really lookin' good, kiddo," Dr. Balis concludes. "We'll start an IV just before your surgery tomorrow morning."

"IV!" Sara gasps. "Dr. J. said no more IV's. I'm getting a line."

"Just one more IV, Sara. We need it to administer the anesthetic when we put the line in."

Sara wears her meanest hospital face, and Dr. Balis worries, "Golly, Sara, you're not going to take my shirt back are you?"

"Not if I can order a root beer."

"I'll let Mike know at the desk."

While she awaits the soft drink, Sara hunts down Nancy

and presents her with the wedding garter.

"Oh Sara," she gushes. "I haven't got one of these yet. And it's so special!"

Sara is sad that she will be in the midst of her transplant on Nancy's wedding day, but our nurse promises photographs of the bride and groom.

"One root beer comin' through," barks Mike, our ward clerk.

While Walt and I unpack and move in, Sara twirls the pop can, reading the label. She whacks her forehead with the palm of her hand and gasps, "The nerve of some people! Sending a child with cancer a product to give her more cancer!" And she twister-butts to the nurses' station, leaving Walt and me wide-eyed in her wake.

Sara smacks the diet pop down in front of Frank Balis. "Can you believe this?" she raves, then reads, " 'Use of this product may be hazardous to your health. This product contains saccharin which has been determined to cause cancer in laboratory animals.' Well, I'm going to give somebody a piece of my mind."

"Go for it, Sara," Frank Balis encourages.

She hightails it to Mike's desk and demands, "Did this root beer come up from the kitchen through the tube?"

"It did," testifies Mike. "Is there something the matter with it?"

"You better believe it," she snorts. "Number one, it's diet pop, and I'm not on a diet. Number two, it causes cancer, and I've already got cancer, ya know."

"Well, it's not my fault, Sara. I just called down for a root beer. Why don't you jot down your complaint and I'll send it back with the pop?"

She fires off a feisty message in large dark cursive, and draws a furious-faced cartoon next to her signature. "Let me know when they send up the apology."

"Will do," smirks Mike.

Sara swaggers past bemused interns, nurses and aides. Sated. Triumphant.

After supper Gayle James and I park on the heater-vent gossip bench while Erin sleeps and Sara and Walt play dominoes. Erin's transplant is July 22, three days before Sara's. Erin's new marrow is a gift from her six-month-old baby brother, Eric, the youngest donor on record. Because they are mismatched, Erin's odds for recovery are only forty percent. We vow to see each other through. "Blood brothers," we joke.

A strange young White Coat shuffles up, clears his throat, and says, "I'm looking for Sara's folks."

"I'm Sara's mom."

"Hi. I'm the resident anesthesiologist, and I need to go over some forms with you and have you sign off for tomorrow's surgery."

"I'll get my husband," I answer. As Gayle and I walk back to the rooms, she elbows me and whispers, "Let me warn you. Don't read 'em, just sign 'em."

Walt and I listen as Black Cloud rumbles over the risks of general anesthesia and surgery. "I suppose," he concludes, "that Sara chances slightly greater danger because of her health problems."

"Health problems," Walt muses. "That's putting it mildly."

"Well," Black Cloud drizzles, "if you'll just read this and sign, I'll head out."

In the morning Dr. Johnson asks Sara if she has any questions about the line or the surgery. "I know pretty much about the line," she boasts. "All my friends have them, you know."

"Of course," he responds.

"And Mom can be with me during the surgery, right?"

"No," Dr. J. regrets. "This is one time Mom can't come along. But you won't even miss her because you'll be asleep. And we'll go ahead and do your bone-marrow aspiration and spinal tap while you're under. How's that?"

She sniffles and worries.

While the nurses transfer drowsy Sara to the gurney for the ride upstairs, she grips my hand and begs, "Don't leave me, Mom."

"Not yet," I answer, and Walt and I walk with her to the double doors of the operating room.

Sara's eyes are trapped-animal eyes as we kiss her good-bye. Then, from inside the Surgical Receiving Window, a familiar voice calls, "Sara Kruckeberg, is that you out there?"

"Carolyn," I shout. "I heard you were working here." I turn to the surgical nurse and explain, "Carolyn is Sara's old playground supervisor."

"How nice," she answers. "I hate to break up the reunion, but we really must be going."

Sara reaches out for me, but Carolyn grabs her hand. "I'll stay right with you, sweetie. Until you're sound asleep."

"That's good," Sara mumbles.

"That's great," I sigh.

Dr. Hickman meets us by the elevator. He says it'll be a few hours. He says get some sunshine and try to relax. He'll take good care of her, he says.

Walt and I stroll University Village. We windowshop Mr. Peeper's Miniatures, dreaming of what fun Sara will have furnishing the doll house Walt built for her last Christmas. "While she's out of school this fall, I'll come home early and we can put together some of these kits," Sara's daddy says.

"She'll love it," I agree.

We buy blue cotton shorty pajamas at Lamont's. "She needs these," I explain to Walt. "Easy to pull on over her line."

"Sure, sure. She really *needs* them."

We grab a burger, then wind up in the COH craft shop. "Look at these babies in the bleach-bottle cradle, Walt. All that handwork, and they're only $4.50."

"And Sara *needs* one. Right?" He shells out the bucks. "Get green, it's her favorite color, now."

When we return to the floor, Mom and Dad and Andy are there. "Hi, honey. Thought we'd help you wait it out," Mama says.

"What a great idea." I hug.

We fluff the flannel quilt a hundred times, pose and repose the new doll bed. Nurse Karen says Sara's in recovery and will be down soon. We sit on the floor outside her room and finally Ed says, "She's on her way."

We meet the gurney by the nurses' station and Grandpa says, "Hi, Beaners."

Sara's eyes open, drift, then focus. "It's Grandpa," she whispers. "I love you, Grandpa."

He nods, squeezes her hand, but doesn't talk. Can't talk.

It's hard to see yesterday's cock-of-the-walk reduced once more to a pale little lump under a sheet.

We cuddle Sara into her bed, examine the entry wound in

her neck, and the line exiting from her chest. "Do you hurt?" I ask.

"A little," she answers. "Thank you for the doll. Green's my favorite color." And she sleeps again.

Dr. Hickman meets us in the hall. "Stoic," he says. "Sara is very stoic."

"She is," I agree.

He details the surgery, never making eye contact, focusing instead on my neck. Self-conscious, I finger my gold chain.

"Excuse me for staring," he apologizes. "But you have a gorgeous exterior jugular. And Sara inherited it."

Mama moseys up. I introduce her to the short, bald, bespectacled Dr. Hickman, and he says, "Pleased to meet you," and pokes at her jugular with a stubby forefinger. "Remarkable," he raves. "It's all in the family."

"He admires our exterior jugulars," I clue Mama.

"Oh, mine always was quite prominent," she chimes.

"Lovely, just lovely. You know, around here they accuse me of never recognizing a face, just a neck. Maybe they're right. Best of luck," he pats my shoulder. "Any problem with that line and you see me."

"He seems like a wonderful man," Mama sighs as we watch Dr. Hickman strut down the hall.

"Man, a little flattery sure goes a long way with you," I tease. And we giggle, massaging our exterior jugulars.

Sara is sore and grouchy the day after surgery. She cries when Jan, the H.A. nurse, cleans the site. "It's not that bad, Sara," Jan reprimands.

"How do you know, you've never had it," Sara wails.

Jan clams up, but continues working. When she finishes, I follow her into the hall. "Is she being a big baby, or does it really hurt?'' I ask.

"Yeah. I guess it's pretty tender the first few days. But in a week or so it won't bother her at all.''

Mom and Dad and Andy visit in the afternoon. Sara displays her new hook-up, details proper care and handling of an H.A. line, and announces she thinks she'll eventually take charge of it all by herself.

"Good for you!'' Grandpa praises.

On brother, I think. Good thing he didn't hear the performance this morning.

Sara banishes me from her room. "Have lunch with Grandma and Grandpa,'' she orders. "Dad and Andy and I have to make some plans for your birthday party. Scram.''

"Do me a favor tomorrow, Daddy,'' I ask in the elevator. "Tomorrow don't ask if I feel any older.''

"It's a deal,'' he answers, and gives my cheek his "beegers-deegers'' pinch. Like he did when I was young.

On July 20, my thirty-fourth birthday, we walk Sara upstairs for an EKG. Cytoxan, the pre-transplant chemotherapy, has numerous possible side effects, heart toxicity among them. Transplant patients are pre- and post-tested. When we return to B-3, Nancy hooks Sara to a fast-drip saline solution in anticipation of this afternoon's Cytoxan infusion. "Less chance of a bladder burn if we really flush it through,'' our nurse explains.

Bakery cake, off-key singing, brown-bagged gifts. Happy birthday to me. From Mom and Dad, a new white sweater to ward off the COH shivers. Andy tosses over new pom-pom socks and Sara says, "Bet I can fit into those.'' Walt clasps a gold chain around my neck as Sara hands me a dinky box fastened with hand-beaded elastic thread. Inside is a gold heart. "I bought it with my own money," she confides. "It means 'I love you'."

As I pull on my new birthday socks, Nancy arrives with the Cytoxan. "Hate to break up the party, but I've got to start this now."

Mom and Dad and Walt and Andy pack for home. My boys will return after the two-day chemotherapy, and our family will enjoy an R and R pass in the 47th Street "bone-marrow house" that COH has for families like us.

"I'll call every morning," Mama promises.

"And I'll call at night," Walt hugs. "Love you, Sissy."

And they're gone again.

"Sara," Nancy says. "I'd like to give Thorazine right along with the Cytoxan."

"You know better than that, Nancy. I can handle it myself."

"Not this you can't, Sara. It's a high dose of strong stuff. Please?"

"No. And that's my final decision."

By dinner time Sara is writhing, retching, begging for relief. "Oh, Mama," she moans, "I'm sorry to do this on your birthday."

Sara wakes a little shaky, a little squeamish and a whole lot anxious to go out on afternoon pass. She refuses breakfast, but brightens when I suggest lunch at University Village.

Bathed, rested, ready to roll, Sara says we'll walk rather

than wait for the shuttle van. She marches, in white shorts and pink Number One Daughter T-shirt, with somber straightforward determination. Sara nods and half-smiles when I point out the drugstore where I walked right into the glass doors and bonked my head, the laundromat where the dryer ate her best pom-pom socks, and the deli where I bought our Sweet Slumber tea. But Sara claps and grins when I point out the COH craft shop, home of the greatest gifts. We charge in and a guild volunteer, charmed by Sara's eager-eyed admiration of the love labors, offers a VIP tour of the back room.

Grey heads bob at sing-song sewing machines, bright yarn balls dance around click-clack knitting needles, lady voices hum over snip-snap pinking shears. This is Santa's workshop. These are Santa's elves.

Sara smooths fabric, pets afghans, rearranges quilt squares, then parks at a table with all the other grandmas. She tells of the special handmade hospital nightie she wore the day of her first admit. She tells how sweet Erin looks in her handmade hospital bonnet. And she tells how baby Cassie lay fingering the handmade hospital quilt the weeks before she died. The ladies listen as Sara talks of handmade healing.

And when we leave, they squeeze our hands and wish us well. We walk away warmed. Loved. Lifted.

Sara's legs wobble when we reach the Village. "I need to rest," she says, so we hoist up on soda-fountain counter stools, eat cheeseburgers, and share a hot-fudge sundae.

Chocolate-charged, we hit the Hallmark shop. Sara wrings her fringed leather Indian purse, agonizing over which posters to buy for her room. "These will be perfect to read every day while I'm in isolation," Sara announces. She unrolls a photograph of a freshly hatched duckling titled, "Arise, go forth, and conquer."

"Perfect," I agree.

"And look at this one, Mama." A beautiful ballerina appears, and Sara reads:

> If you can imagine it, you can achieve it.
> If you can dream it, you can become it.

"For sure," I say. "Pay for them and let's get out of here."

We decide to hitch back to the hospital via the shuttle van. Sara chatters away as we bounce by University Hospital, then loop back to Sand Point Way. "This reminds me of the Anaheim Fun Bus," she prattles. "What was your favorite ride again, Mom? Pirates of the Caribbean, or Small World? I keep forgetting."

"Remember?" I sigh. "I liked them both the same. One for excitement and one for relaxation."

"Right," she says.

As we cruise up the long driveway to the COH entrance, a woman turns and smiles, "Excuse me. Are you Sara, by any chance?" Sara nods. "I'm Frank Balis's wife and I pretty much recognized you from his description. Then when you talked about Disneyland I just had to ask for sure. Our little boy has worn Frank's Mickey Mouse shirt to bed every night. What a wonderful gift, Sara."

"Well, actually he hinted for it, you know," Sara confides as she hops off the bus. And Mrs. Balis laughs.

"You have a wonderful husband," I say, following Sara out the door.

"And you have a lovely daughter. I'm glad I met her. Best of luck," wishes our new friend.

I hang posters as Nurse Karen begins the Cytoxan infusion. "Have the Thorazine ready," Sara orders. "I'll let you know when I need it."

"Sounds good, Sara. Whenever you say."

As the drip begins, Lori arrives. She is the oldest daughter of our close friends, the Verstegens. Our "other family." Recently graduated from the University of Washington, Lori works in Seattle, but visits her folks often. She is a Sequim connection. Tonight she brings homebaked cookies, hometown newspapers, and a little homegrown gossip. "Can't stay," she says. "David's waiting in the lobby."

"We'll walk you down," Sara offers. "I need a cruise." Lori and I cluck over her husband David's new haircut. Sara studies, frowns, pronounces it "punk," then offers him her scarf. In the middle of our belly laughs, Sara stands and announces, "We need to head back."

"Are you sick?" I worry.

"Almost," she answers. And we're off.

"I need it now, Karen," Sara bustles past the nurses' station.

"Comin' up," sighs Karen, hot on our trail.

The night noises—dry heaves, soft moans, clanking puke pans—pass by midnight, and Sara sleeps until seven. She wakes up pale but perky, glad to be done with the drug. "That's the worst of it, Sara," says Nancy. "Things get easier now. We'll flush you good today, and if you don't have any bladder burn by this afternoon, you'll be all set for a two-day pass."

We spend the day in the hallway agonizing with Gayle and

Rick James. A routine pre-op physical exam turned up a heart murmur in baby Eric, Erin's donor, and he faces increased risk from anesthesia. "This is a fine time to tell us," Gayle sobs. "The radiation is wiping Erin out right now. What're we supposed to do?"

"We'll go ahead with it, Gayle," smooths Dr. Johnson. "But we are obligated to make you aware of this new twist."

While Rick paces in the smoking lounge, Gayle slumps in a corner, head on her knees. Sara and I take turns patting her back.

Walt and Andy arrive and I snatch Walt into a corner and fall apart. "I can't stand any more of this," I wail.

"Settle down right now." Walt holds me. "And remember, your energy belongs to Sara."

"We're all packed," I sigh. "We've got our pass papers and the key to the house on 47th Street. Let's get out of here."

"Well, *The Daily News* guys are meeting us here any time now. Remember?"

"We'll leave them directions to the house."

"No way, Carol. It was your idea to have them see this hospital and get their facts from Dr. Johnson. We'll wait right here."

I haul into the bathroom, pull on my Super Mom T-shirt and smile my Donna Reed smile.

The news reporters arrive with flowers for Sara, and I know they are too young to understand all this. But what else is new? Sara shies, Andy mauls Walt, and my armpits are soaked. Finally Sara loosens up and fires off a few corkers.

Yes, she's glad her Dad's a match. She'll take his marrow, but he can keep his whiskers, thank you anyway.

Boy, Dad's always tellin' her to be brave for the pokes.

Now it's his turn and she hopes they get him good.

No, she doesn't spend a lot of time worrying about the transplant. "I don't see that we had a decision to make," she shrugs. "I've lived through everything before and that's all I can say."

Ralph rolls in to explain the technical procedures, and spends a lot of time pasting down his cowlick as the camera click-click-clicks.

Finally finished, *The Daily News* reporters promise to tour the facilities and talk with Dr. J. They shake our hands and wish us well. "We'll check back Friday. Be cool, Sara."

"Well, they weren't exactly like Clark Kent," Sara giggles when they're out of earshot. "But they were pretty nice."

"Right," we agree, and we're off to the bone-marrow house. Nestled two blocks from COH, it is spacious and homey. Closets crammed with toys, coffee tables heaped with magazines, cupboards stocked with staples, notes of love and cheer left by previous tenants.

The kids play in the sun room while Walt and I nose around. We find messages from Denise, Marge, Becky and Helen.

"Peace to all who enter."

"If you need to talk, call Helen." Followed by a Maryland phone number.

A calendar entry, "Becky flies home in three more days. Yippee!"

Walt and I laugh, imagining our friends and their kids under this same roof.

I make up beds and Walt brings hamburgers in for supper. Then, bathed and storied, the kids are tucked into twin beds.

We hit the streets early Wednesday morning, flush Sara's

H.A. line in clinic, breakfast downtown, then head for the zoo. The kids ride the Shetlands and Walt laughs at Sara's long thin legs, hanging almost to the ground, as she sways round the riding ring atop her little pony.

After the zoo, we take in *The Empire Strikes Back*, then mosey home for spaghetti dinner.

Sara is restless and fussy this evening. She picks on Andy, tapes and retapes her H.A. dressing, wants to sleep with extra bulldog clamps in case blood backs into her line. "One is enough, Sara," I sigh. "Good night."

When she finally wrestles off to sleep, it is my turn to search out the sand man.

We are all shot in the morning, and decide to breakfast at a restaurant before returning to COH.

"Mr. Kruckeberg? Remember me?" Our waitress is one of Walt's old students.

"Sure. Nice to see you, Susan," he greets her.

"Do you still teach in Sequim? Are you guys over here on vacation or something?"

"Not exactly," mutters Walt. "Sara's being treated for cancer at Children's Orthopedic."

"Oh," gulps poor Susan. "I'll be right back to take your order."

We choke down bacon and eggs. Sara stirs her food, cries, and says she might vomit. We leave a big tip and rush for fresh air.

We tidy the house, wash the sheets and pack our bags. Sara wants to go back to the hospital, read her mail, visit her friends. Settle in.

Walt snaps her picture in the COH parking lot. "Soak up the sunshine, Sissy," Walt teases. "Last time you'll feel it for a few weeks.''

She takes big deep breaths, King Kongs her chest and cart-wheels back to B-3.

We party in the evening, eat popcorn, fresh fruit and chips. Our home movies entertain Grandma and Grandpa, staff and patients—entertain everyone except Sara.

Head down, eyes up, she charges the floor, rippling, snort-ing, pawing turf. When my folks and Andy start for the ferry dock, Sara begs them to stay longer.

"Sleep, Beaners," Grandpa says. "We'll talk to you to-morrow night."

But Beaners won't sleep. Can't sleep. She bounces in and out of bed. Back and forth to the bathroom. Heart racing. Pulse pounding. "I keep having to pee," she wails. "Oh Mama, I have to pee again."

Past midnight, I ask that Sara be sedated, but the intern on call won't do it. "Then let him sleep down here with her," I fume.

When I return, Sara is quiet and Walt snores in a chair beside her bed.

We are restless tonight. The transplant, her donor, and me.

Walt and I wake early and roll right out. We need to escape our heads.

July 25. The final assault. Hit the beaches. T-Day.
Confused and shy. How do we greet this day? With de-

spair and desperation? With joy and celebration?

Sara lies still and stoic for a final blood draw. She doesn't give her usual guff when the Thorazine is administered. As the drug takes hold, I cuddle her as I always do. Once again, Nancy outlines the agenda.

Sara and Nancy will travel by ambulance to the basement of the Fred Hutchinson Cancer Center, where Sara will undergo total body radiation. Sara will lie in a small room. Alone. Nancy will watch over her via closed-circuit television. Sara will be sedated throughout the day. She will be nauseated and vomit, but if she can take care of herself, the machine can keep running and the time will go faster. "I can do it, Nancy," Sara promises.

"But if you need me, Sara, if you want me, I'll be there in a second," Nancy assures her.

Sara smiles, sleepy, "That's good, Nancy."

"It's kinda chilly in the room, Sara. Sometimes that makes you less nauseous."

"I hate being cold, Nancy. May I bring my quilt?"

"Sure," answers Sara's surrogate sister.

The ambulance attendants wait quietly in the hall. As Nancy gathers her sweater and purse, they quickstep in, transfer Sara to the gurney, strap her down, and we kiss goodbye. "See you soon, Sissy. We love you."

"Love you too," she drowses, and closes her eyes. Walt walks her to the elevator, but I cry on the heater vent and worry about what we've done.

Walt returns. "God, I'm starved." We hug and laugh at his gut reaction to every crisis.

"Too bad, big boy," I remind him. "No breakfast for you." Walt goes to surgery early this afternoon and may not eat until after he returns.

The anesthesiologist finds Walt, who elects to have a spinal block, consent forms are signed, and we hit the cafeteria. Walt looks on as I savor each morsel.

"Snap to it," Walt growls. "Let's go for a walk."

We head down Sand Point Way and end up at the COH craft shop, fingering the hand-sewn rag dolls that are too expensive.

"Sara loved this one," I say, holding a carefully crafted infant doll posed on hands and knees. "She named it Crawly Baby."

"Twenty bucks. We'll buy it. Money goes for a good cause. What color?" Walt fires.

"Pink for Sara. And this one for Nikki—she's our new neighbor."

Walt grins. "Great idea." We drop forty dollars, and make a quick get-away. We know we can't buy off Sara's pain, but that doesn't keep us from trying.

The morning sun is hot. We sweat on down to University Village to buy new Jockey shorts. I don't want Walt going to surgery trussed in tattletale greys.

Back on B-3, the nurses have emptied Sara's room. Our custodian, Cora, disinfects the floor, walls, bathroom and furniture. I sit on the hall carpet and wipe down Sara's books and toys. Dr. Johnson questions the necessity of this task, but it gives a mom something to do. Walt paces and bitches about his hunger pangs, but brightens when he spies my sister Jane. They talk tennis and volleyball until interrupted by a Valium.

Though Walt insists he is already relaxed, he grudges the little white pill down the hatch. The resident anesthesiologist smiles, "Good boy."

Thirty minutes later, a surgical aide arrives with the wheel-chair to escort the patient to the fourth floor. "I'll walk," grumbles Walt. Since Walt is the oldest patient admitted to COH in many a moon, there is much good-natured bantering as he drifts by B-3's receiving desk. We arrive on Surgery to a flurry of flustered nurses. Alas. There are no surgical nighties in Walt's size. He is ushered into the doctors' dressing room. When he emerges, he is garbed in a green surgeon's gown. As Walt weaves through the double doors, I'm proud of the snowy white thirty-sixes flapping in the breeze.

The endless afternoon begins. Jane suggests a Red Robin taco salad, followed by our annual birthday underpants ex-change. The nurses encourage us to have a good time and to hustle back before shift change so they can admire our pur-chases.

On a holiday high, we sip Margaritas with our salads, then giggle on down to Lamont's lingerée department. I buy black lace. She loves the leopards. Singing "Happy Birthday To You," we exchange sacks, and sober up for the reality of our return.

My big sister, who's sat through every trauma of my life, sits with me now. Drinking machine coffee. Waiting. The call comes from the Hutch. Sara is on her way back.

They wheel her quickly into 313, sleeping, vomiting, flushed. The isolation sign is slapped on her door. I mask, and stand guard beside her bed.

Sara has radiation sunburn, high fever, sick stomach and swollen parotid glands. Nancy says she was a trooper. Her nausea is subsiding, but her neck will be enlarged for a day or two. She should feel pretty good by this evening.

Jane masks and reports that the first bag of marrow is on its way. Nancy hangs it, hooks it up, and we sing praises and snap pictures of this promise of new life entering Sara's blood stream.

Walt is in recovery, and will be made comfortable in the dialysis room down the hall in an hour or so.

Nancy, exhausted, smooths Sara's nightgown and leaves us to Karen, the tenderest of B-3's nurses. We share "Sara stories," while Karen monitors temperature, pulse, blood pressure and heart rate. Sara stirs and asks, "How's Daddy?"

"Part of him is right here with you," I joke. And she smiles up at the bright red bag.

"A lot of pokes," she says before dozing off. Ed, the ward clerk, comes on the intercom to tell us that Walt is down from recovery.

"Auntie Jane and Karen are here, Sissy. You talk to them while I go to see Daddy," I whisper.

"Tell him hi for me," she smiles.

Walt is stretched out stiff in a curtained-off corner of the dialysis room. "How ya doin', honey?" I croon.

"OK," he woozes. "A little headache and incredible pressure on my back."

"I think that's to be expected."

"Carol, I just know it'd be better if I could get my shorts off, but my legs are still numb."

"Who put your shorts back on?"

"The nurses," he grins. "It took three of them."

With prune-faced disapproval, I uncover Walt and proceed to remove his underwear. "I usually get better cooperation when I do this," I chastize.

"Can the corn, Carol. Just get 'em off."

I gasp. "These are *not* your new Jockeys!" I accuse. "Just how did you lose your brand-new shorts, Walt?"

He groans as I wrestle the strangers down over his thighs. Between thumb and forefinger I dangle somebody else's cute little thirty-twos. "No wonder it took three nurses," I mumble.

And I know then that somewhere, in a secret stash, there stands a bronzed pair of spanking-new thirty-sixes labeled, "Biggest shorts ever admitted to COH."

As the last of Walt's marrow mainlines into Sara's artery, she's fevered, mucus-mouthed and anxious to see her daddy. Jane says she'll deliver the message on her way out. My sister and I squeeze goodbye, working hard to bite the bullet. But when she says she's so proud of me, I bawl all over her blouse. She rocks me, ruffles my hair, rubs my back. And once again, I'm five years old, just been spanked. Seventh grade and still no chest. Dateless sweet sixteen. "It'll be OK," she says, as she always says. "We'll wash your face with a nice cold cloth."

In a little while, Walt masks and limps in to lie with his little girl. Dr. Johnson joins us to give Sara a once-over. "Have you got the mumps, girl?" he teases, touching Sara's swollen parotid glands.

"I hate all this mucus," she gripes, spitting into a Kleenex.

"That's a radiation side effect, sweetheart. And it won't last long, I promise. You all get some rest. I'll pop by first thing tomorrow."

Walt and Sara share late-night television while I crash on

the bed. "I don't know why she's so tired," Sara whispers. "She didn't have to do anything today."

"That's for sure," agrees Walt.

"You bums," I hiss, not opening my eyes. "While you slept the day away, I was in charge of worrying. And that takes a lot out of a guy."

They laugh, but I don't think they're funny.

In the morning, Sara's glands are less swollen, but she has filled a waste can with mucusy Kleenex. Tired of fetching fresh tissues, Nurse Marshall directs me to the supply room. "Feel free," she says. When I return with a stash, Sara is designing the special notices that must appear on a transplant's door.

MASKS AND GOOD HANDWASHING REQUIRED is tricolor printed.

IRRADIATE ALL BLOOD PRODUCTS sports a blue-faced, claw-toothed Dracula peeking out from a bottom corner.

And detailed pictures of blood-draw equipment adorn R.N.'S DO ALL BLOODWORK.

"The snazziest signs we've ever had on B-3," raves Marshall.

Walt needs to reassure Andy, in person, that all is well, so after his discharge, he touches cheeks with Sara—it's hard to kiss through a mask—and starts for home.

Isolation begins as an adventure. "Take the Polaroid," says Sara, "and snap a picture of everybody in a natural pose. I'll hang them on my wall and it'll be just like they're here with me."

"Great idea," I say, and rip out with the camera.

"Natural pose," muses Nurse Karen. "Well here I am, sweet and unassuming." Click.

"I naturally eat a lot," says Don the aide, stuffing a cupcake down his gullet. Click.

"I'm a natural hard worker," boasts Ed, hiding a novel under the desk. He picks up the telephone and shuffles papers. Click.

"I just do what comes naturally," slouches Adrian, knees up, bug-eyed, gap-mouthed in a wheelchair. With a finger up his nose. Click.

Sara, the film critic, pronounces the prints "a little on the darkish side" but adequate. "Too bad Adrian turned out at all." But she slaps him up smack in the middle of her wall.

Sunday, Bill comes to visit and brings Sara a pig poster. They hold it between them and I photograph the pair pointing at one another. "I love it when Uncle Bull comes," Sara smiles as he snorts out the door. "Will Auntie Nan come again, soon? She makes me laugh."

Sara thrives on visits from relatives. If she's bored, uncles play, if she's sad, aunties cheer up. When she talks, cousins listen. Cousins, with self-assigned roles. Mary, the spiritual advisor. Jennifer, B-313's interior decorator. Joe, the stand-up comedian. Sara's closest cousin, Angie. And the four-year-old social director, Uncle Bill's Carrie.

"I'll call Auntie Nan and see," I promise.

In the morning, Todd Pearson, our transplant intern, masks and strolls in the door. "How's it going, Sara? Any complaints?" he asks as he scrubs his hands.

She growls.

"How's your bottom? Still itchy?"

"Maybe yes. Maybe no."

Radiation irritates delicate membranes, and Sara's bottom is tops on her list of complaints. Even so, she hates having handsome Dr. Pearson "taking a peek."

"Roll over for me, Sara. I'll be real speedy. We just have to make sure no infection gets started there."

Until Walt's marrow grafts, any infection can be lethal. Sara knows this, grudges onto her side, and bares her butt.

When Walt calls tonight he is incredulous. The Benefit Dance for Sara, sponsored by our friends, has snowballed into the social event of the season. Printed tickets, four bands, food, drink, door prizes. Every reader board in town proclaims:

> DANCE FOR SARA
> August 2   9:00   VFW

Sequim is electric, Walt says, and he feels the charge.

"Hey, you don't need to tell me about it. We're lit up clear over here. Sara's supposed to be wiped out and she bebops all day long. No IV, no antibiotics, no nothing. Energized," I say. "They are powerful people."

"God, I want to see her," Walt sighs. "We'll be over tomorrow even if we have to stay in a motel."

"That's great, Walt. It'll be good to have us all together again. And I want to tell you all about the Clines."

They came out west to strike it rich. They came out west to escape the dust bowl of relapse with no more remission. They came out west in a crumpled station wagon, heaped with prayers and promises. Praise the Lord! Rough, ready and reborn. The Clines from Ohio.

Nikki's bone-marrow transplant isolation is prolonged by an early onset of graft-versus-host disease. Her new marrow immediately rejects its host.

In turn, Nikki rejects her family's attempt to exorcise the sagging spirit from her wracked body. While her parents, Barb and Roger, sing scripture, warmed with the Word, Nikki studies pigeons.

On the ledge outside the window, a pair of pigeons share watch over four eggs. They began building the scraggly nest the day of Nikki's admission to B-3. They laid eggs the day of her transplant. And the countown begins.

With unwavering faith, the Clines and the pigeons await emergence of new life. Patients, parents and staff don masks and enter Nikki's room. We peer at her pigeons and her parents. We ooh and ahh at such unrelenting optimism. Perched precariously on a narrow ledge in a crumbling nest, the piegons and the Clines stand steady. Their cooing calms us.

Today Nikki ventures out of isolation and wobbles into the hallway. When she returns to her room, four bald baby birds squeak a triumphant welcome. B-3 reverberates with the evangelics of Roger Cline. "Hallelujah! We shall be released!"

The preacher man noses up to our window. "Rejoice, pretty Sara," jump-shouts Roger Cline. "Your daddy and your brother-boy are a-comin' down the hall. Right now this very minute!"

Sara smiles and waves. She loves Roger and the rambunctious routine he brings to her isolation. Every night he bounces in at nine. "Goin' for pizza, gorgeous girl. What'll it be?"

Every night she grins, "One piece of pepperoni with black olives, please."

Every night he asks, "How 'bout you, Mama?"

Every night I answer, "None for me, thanks."

"Not one itty bitty bite?"

"Not tonight."

Every night, when the pizza arrives, Sara says, "I guess I'm really not very hungry, Mama. Can you eat it?"

And, every night, I do.

Our boys mask and whisk in the door. Walt hugs, rolls his eyes and says, "That guy is a brick short of a load. He grabbed me outside the elevator and said, 'God love ya, brother. It's good to have ya among us.' How do you deal with him?"

The image of the two hulks embracing makes me laugh, and I say I love him because Sara loves him.

While Nancy takes vital signs, Andy riffles through Sara's latest treasures, rattling off neighborhood-kid messages. "Oh, Andy," Sara scolds. "You spray when you talk and your mask is all soggy."

"I know," he mourns, his brown eyes flooding. "And I can't breathe good, either."

Nancy squeezes his meaty little shoulders and says she has a plan. There are some heavy-duty masks with elastic backs. Comfortable, sturdy and expensive. She'll pirate a box just for Andy.

Our gratitude embarrasses Nancy out the door. "No biggie," she shrugs. "Just don't waste them, Andy."

When Nancy's gone, I tell Walt that since Rick and Gayle James occupy the main floor of the 47th Street house, he and Andy must sack out in the basement. The new social worker will bring us the key this afternoon.

We fritter away the day. Walt and Sara visit, play games and snooze while Andy and I rec-room, eat and chatter. By evening Andy's walled in and wild-eyed. Walt's not far behind.

"We'd better hit it," Walt says. "You got the key?"

"*I* haven't got it. Didn't the social worker bring it to the room?"

"No," Walt snaps. "We'd better have her paged."

"She won't be here this late. Why didn't you mention the key before this?"

"You're the one who made the arrangements," Walt says.

"Well, you're the one who needs the house," I counter. "Besides, it's no catastrophe. Just knock on the upstairs door. Gayle and Rick will let you in."

"Right." Walt grudges a goodbye kiss and piggybacks his boy down the hall.

I pace the living room outside 313, too tired to sleep.

"Sara tucked in?" Erin's grandma whispers. I look at the little lady decked out in hair curlers, flannel nightie and tired eyes, and start to cry. "Oh, Carol," she joins me. "I know. I know. It's so hard, isn't it?"

"Yeah," I hiccup. "And Walt and I just had a stupid fight over a stupid key." I heave out the whole stupid story.

"Oh, dear," Grandma worries. "And Gayle and Rick aren't there this evening."

"You're kidding," I wail just as Walt and Andy reappear on the scene.

"No one's home." Walt glares.

"They're at Rick's sister's house," Grandma mutters. "They'll be back by eleven or eleven-thirty."

"We'll sleep in the car until they get back," Walt sighs. I cry harder and Grandma checks on Erin.

We pacify Andy with a popsicle and I plead with Walt to sleep on a cot in the hospital schoolroom tonight. "I'm sure we can sneak Andy in just for one night."

As Walt massages his puffy eyes with the palms of his hands, considering my alternative, Erin's grandma returns, robed and smiling. "I just called Rick's sister's house. The kids left twenty minutes ago. They should be almost home by now."

"Good news." Walt thanks her, and I walk my weary boys to the fourth-floor exit.

The days are long and hard for Andy-boy, and by Thursday he needs his own bed. In the parking lot I ask Walt if he'll attend Sara's Benefit Dance. "I've thought about it a lot. And Carol, I just don't think I can do it. Will people think I'm rude and ungrateful? Should I make myself go?"

"No. I couldn't go either," I confess. "People will understand."

"Besides," Walt jabs me, his wife with two left feet. "Who would I dance with if you weren't there?"

We kiss goodbye and I watch them coast down the hill for home.

"Sandy, Carol and Rita called while you were gone," Sara announces. "They'll all call back. Rita says there's a huge banner hanging above the V.F.W. and it says in humongous letters, DANCE FOR SARA, and she's gonna take pictures of everything for me. Carol says everybody in Sequim knows me, but she thinks I picked a dumb way to get famous. And Sandy says Garland's band is practicing up to play 'The Gambler,' and she'll record it, but it won't sound quite like Kenny." Sara takes a big breath, then smiles that gentle serene smile I've come to know so well. "We are lucky people, aren't we, Mama?"

"Very lucky," I agree. And I'm surprised that I mean it.

By Saturday supper, all of B-3 knows what's cooking at the V.F.W. in Sequim, Washington tonight. Marshall waltzes in with the meal tray, Adrian twirls in a bath-towel tutu, and Barb and Roger Cline fox trot past Sara's window. "Corn-y!" Sara moans, but her eyes dance faster than her whirling friends.

Walt calls just past the ten o'clock rate change. "You've got to hear this," he says. He hangs the phone out our dining-room window, and it's as if I'm on hold, hearing that faint background music. "Can you believe it?" Walt says. "I didn't need to go to the dance. The dance came to me."

The V.F.W. is three blocks from our house. The music rides the close August evening air. "Listen, Sissy." I pull the phone to her bedside. She lies on her pillow and listens a long time. Smiling. Dancing.

My husband and I talk on and on into the night. Sara dozes to the drone. We affirm and reaffirm that all is well. Walt was a match, a minor miracle for sure. But all these people directing all that energy must be the very greatest miracle. "If love conquers all," Walt concludes, "we've got it made in the shade."

At 1:00 a.m. the phone rings again. It's Rita and Auntie Nan from the pay phone at the V.F.W. "It's a happening," Rita shouts. "People are here from all over the world. It's too crowded to dance."

"Doug won the TV," Nan chimes in, "and turned it back

for the mayor to auction off. This town is incredible. Even your sister Jane is ready to move to Sequim. She's decided small-town life can be pretty special."

"Everybody's autographed the banner," Rita yells. "We'll get it over to you. Aubrey and I dug through the dumpster trying to find the ticket stubs for an accurate count and the names of the people who are here, but we packed it in when the Greyhound came through the alley spotlighting Aubrey hanging on to my heinie so I wouldn't fall into the garbage."

"Oh, I wish I could've seen it," I laugh. "Tell me more."

"Bob and Chuck are manhandling women on the dance floor. Coach Finley ripped out country western like nobody's business, and here comes a bunch of California yacht owners right off the street!"

"We love you," my sisters and my friends shout. "Kiss Sara goodnight."

"We love you too. I'll call for more details tomorrow. But not too early."

I do not sleep tonight. My head dances.

In the morning I tell Sara of the wee-hours phone call. She's still chortling when I flick on "CBS Sunday Morning."

"This morning we bring you the tale of a modern-day Job and his family," Charles Kuralt intones. "Stricken with a modern-day pestilence—cancer. When we return."

I move to hit the switch, but Sara says to stop. She wants to watch.

The feature tells of a midwestern family under siege. One son dead of leukemia, one son paralyzed by cancer treatment, a third child rejoicing in remission. And a father struggling with his own cancer diagnosis.

Sara is riveted to our tiny television screen. She eats,

swims, talks and laughs with the family. Her family. And when the mother answers, "No, we have no time for bitterness . . . we say a prayer for every good moment we share," the camera fades out on her soft wise smile. And I look at my little girl nodding, smiling back.

"Oh, Mama," she says, stroking her quilt. "And we think we've got troubles."

Sunday evening, Walt says he can't stand the separation any longer. He and Andy are moving to Seattle. Find an apartment, a motel, anything. They'll be here Wednesday. Sara and I study classifieds, chase down leads, and Tuesday evening the social worker brings good news. The second transplant house, on 20th Street, is vacant and waiting for our boys. The cost is five dollars a day and a free-will offering of TLC. One house is owned by COH, the other by COH Oncology Department funding; both are maintained by the Washington State Candle-lighters—parents and relatives of childhood cancer patients.

Walt is packing when I call to report the accommodations. He promises to be here in time to take me to Fred Hutchinson, where I will donate plasma. Dr. Johnson says that a small percentage of women who have borne two or more children have antibodies that are essential for transplant typing. I am one of them, and would I donate?

Would I? Would I? I close my eyes to fantasize. And for one brief moment I am a walking gold mine. A key factor in cancer research. A wonder drug.

Wednesday morning Sara is angry. She does not want me to leave, and why can't Daddy stay with her. Or at least Andy

She'll survive a few hours alone, I say, gentle but firm. By the time Walt picks me up, she's hysterical and I'm mad. "You're a big girl," I fume. "Get hold of yourself."

"Just go," Nancy orders. "I'll deal with her."

"What's the matter with Sissy?" Andy worries on the way to the car.

"She's just got a little cabin fever," I tell him. "She'll be fine." But my stomach churns.

Fred Hutchinson Cancer Center juts up from Seattle's Pill Hill. Walt and Andy escort me to the H.L.A. lab, find out it's a ninety-minute process, then head for breakfast.

I complete an extended family history form, then the technician explains the two-part process. The drawn blood filters through a machine that extracts plasma from whole blood. The red cells are held, then transfused back into the vein. The needle, she says, is a little larger than the standard blood-donor variety, and when she asks, "Does it hurt?" I lie and say no. I want to cry for all the times Sara's been stabbed and I've commanded, "Be brave."

During the procedure I lie in a lounge chair and the tech asks if I'm interested in an H.L.A. typing lesson. When I say sure, she smiles, "Great. I'll get the Kruckeberg file." I understand twenty-five percent of her scientific details, but I understand one hundred percent of her commitment to the welfare of my family. She talks of Andy, Walt and Sara as old buddies, and she says she participated in our typing. When she asks if I've a picture of Sara, I'm amazed to think she knows so much about my daughter but has never seen her face.

After replacing the red cells, my new friend asks if I'd like to see the Hutch transplant facility. "I was going to ask," I reply. "Dr. Johnson calls your methods 'Star Wars medicine.' "

"Oh he does, does he," she chuckles.

The transplant wing is a narrow-halled unit decorated with portraits of bone-marrow-transplant successes. It feels precise, clinical but not cold. Patients are sealed in sterile air-flow units, fed sterilized food, and visiting family must don sterile gowns, caps, masks, gloves and boots. There are no parent sleep-in facilities. Despite these precautions, Hutch transplants have no higher a success rate than those done at COH.

The communal kitchen in the center of the floor is bright white light, gingham tablecloths, families hustling lunch. The friendliest spot on the floor.

At the elevator I thank my guide and scurry off to share my morning with Walt. The boys wrestle on the crew-cut lawn. "How was it?" Walt pants, warding off a sneak attack.

In the car I detail my experiences, concluding, "a nice place to visit, but I'm glad we don't live there."

We pull up at home, COH, B-313, and stumble in on high times. Nancy and Sara are cross-legged on the bed, surrounded by construction paper, scissors and glue. "Look at my Miss Piggy!" Nancy shrieks. "And I never thought I was artistic. Sara did Kermit. I'll probably get fired, but I'm so proud of this pig. Would you mind taking a Polaroid, Walt? So I can show Don."

Sara laughs, circles with her index finger at the side of her head, then points at Nurse Nancy, who nudges the little smart alec and says, "See if I spend another morning with you."

"I didn't mean it. I didn't mean it," giggles Sara, hugging her best friend.

"I should hope not," sniffs Nancy. "Now smile for the picture. I've got to get some work done today."

After the snapshots and a short visit, Walt and Andy head

out to move into the 20th Street house. They'll return after Andy's nap, and I'll drive over for inspection. Sara says it's nice to be a together family again and did we remember that it was her birthday tomorrow?

"You're kidding!" teases Walt. "Well, I guess I've got some shopping to do." And our boys are off and running.

Late afternoon Walt spells me in 313 while I take Andy birthday shopping. He chooses a hand-quilted purse from the COH craft shop. Then we buzz to the bone-marrow house. I can't believe how great it feels to vacuum, make beds and swish out the toilet bowl. "I've gone bonkers!" I squeeze Andy, and he pulls away with a worried wrinkly face that makes me laugh louder.

Buying cake mix at the supermarket, I bump into Dr. Sarah Wright, an intern on hematology service. She is a rabbit, skittering the aisles, clutching a basket of fresh blueberries. "Oh," she gasps, grabbing my arm. "This is the last basket of fresh blueberries and I've got to have them, but I'm short a few cents."

"Here's a dollar. Keep the change," I laugh.

"Thank you," she smiles and zips off to the check-out.

Our family lazes away the evening in Sara's room, playing Mad Libs, watching TV and dealing Uno. When Andy loses and throws the cards on the floor, Walt hoists him up and heads home. "See you bright and early, birthday baby." He kisses Sissy farewell. "And put a book on your butt. Nine hacks can be plenty painful."

Sara sleeps with a smile tonight.

Dr. Sarah ignores the hand-fashioned *verboten* posted on our window: Extreme Caution! Wild Animal Inside! She sallies in undaunted. It is 6:45 a.m., and Sara stretches awake to the scent of blueberry muffins and a whispery rendition of "Happy Birthday To You."

"There are millions of muffins!" Sara exclaims, and Dr. Sarah modestly admits that they are still warm. She tumbled out at 5:30 to bake them. She adds that Sara may offer one to anybody who stops by to sing happy birthday. And then the doctor-girl twinkles away with her special secret. Today Sara will feed every intern in Children's Orthopedic.

It is day fourteen of the transplant. Sara's marrow has bottomed out. She has low platelets, decreased red cells and no white count. Sara's spirits runneth over. She has big dreams, high hopes and all the faith.

I whip away my mask to sneak a peck. "Brush your teeth and find your undies," Sara admonishes. "Get ready for rounds." It is August 7, Sara is nine, and the world waits. I hop to it, charged by her vitality. While I dress, Grandpa phones from home. His traditional off-key, "and many moooooore," is a heartfelt prayer this year.

Walt and Andy, Sara's favorite masked men, rumble over from the 20th Street house. Andy piles on to Sara's bed, cartoons blare, and the game goes on. They choose up superheroes, flick off the TV set, and begin their own dynamic dialogue. As Walt and I head for breakfast, we share a look of mock concern. Once again, Sara has finagled our five-year-old macho man into the role of Electra Woman. His falsetto is starting to ring true.

Over watery scrambled eggs and steamy coffee, Walt tells me he has defied my order. He bought Sara the too-extravagant tape deck. He doesn't care if he spoils her. So there. My sputter cools to simmer. Like everything else these days, Walt is out of my control.

Resigned, I share the complete handmade Barbie Doll wardrobe Andy and I purchased from the craft shop. As Walt fingers the beading on the bridal gown, we laugh at how we once affirmed that *our* daughter would never own any of those sexist bosomy broads. Were we ever so young and foolish?

Returning to B-3, we discuss the party. I will zip over to 20th Street and decorate the birthday cake this morning. We'll nap the kids after lunch, then whoop it up this afternoon. The best-laid plans . . .

Rounds have arrived at 313. The doctors, decked in horned hats, are singing accidental harmony, stuffing mouthfuls of muffins under their masks. Sara directs the choir, waving a bouquet of huge helium balloons sent by the Borgstroms. Her giggly face is testimony to the button someone has taped to her nightie, "I'm happy 'cause today's my birthday!" Andy bounces on the hide-a-bed. He is higher than the balloons.

Nurses cluck outside the door, and kind Cora waits, mop in hand, ready to spiff up the birthday bedroom.

"Poor Cora," I apologize. "We make your job tough."

"Child," she croons, "I'll smile on this sight all day long. That's love in there, girl. That's love."

Ralph snags me into a corner. He has arranged for Sara to leave isolation for her party this afternoon. The weather is warm, and the staff feels there is little chance of infection if Sara sucks in the wide open spaces for an hour. Hospital security will be up at two to unhitch the alarm system on the fire door. We will surprise Sara, and celebrate her ninth birthday on the third-floor fire escape.

My farewell is stifled by the hullabaloo in 313. I am off to create a culinary masterpiece. I have designed a cake shaped like a big bone. The cupcakes sitting on top represent polys, the mature infection-fighting white cells Sara is awaiting. Since Sara's polys will be from Walt's marrow, the cupcakes sport curly black licorice hair and mustache.

The 20th Street house is steamy, but I whistle while I work because this cake is clever, keen, a divine inspiration. I am eager to entertain the inevitable raves. While I frost, I practice acceptance: a serene smile and unassuming shrug.

The cake completed, I center it on a foil-covered board, secure it to the back seat of the Oldsmobile and ease on down the road.

The bank thermometer blinks 84° as I idle at a stoplight on Sand Point Way. I cast an admiring glance at the back seat, and find the Walt-cloned cupcakes melted face down on the floor. In the glow of a green light, to the tune of ten thousand horns, I lovingly lift those babies back onto the bone.

By the time I reach the hospital, the bone looks as if it's been bitten and buried. But my friends are good friends. They oooh and aaah and take pictures of my cake. And Sara reacts with all the righteous indignation I had hoped for. She loves telling strangers she will grow black curly hair and a mustache from her father's marrow, but heaven help us if we tease her about such a possibility.

She watches wistfully as we set up her party on the balcony. She accepts that glass will separate her from her guests. And when Ralph arrives to escort her out the door, Sara won't budge.

Finally assured it's no joke, she minces into the hall,

glances guilty to the right, furtive to the left, then scampers to the fire escape and freedom. Her interns, nurses, friends and family follow.

The tiny cement circle glitters with wall-to-wall joy. Sara opens a miniature birthday cake for her dollhouse, satiny grown-up Bikini panties, rolls of snazzy Hallmark stickers, a new bald Barbie Doll with five wigs, and pierced ear rings for some day.

Sara surveys the ribbons, the wrappings, the gifts, the friends, the family, the love that surrounds her, squeezes her hovering brother and whispers, "Oh Andy, this is my best birthday ever."

And we look away from the defenseless, skinny little bald girl. And we look away from each other until we can get it together again.

It's bedtime now, and the lights are out. My daughter and I are alone with the memory of Walt wearing Hallmark sticker lips on his mask and Andy feeding birthday cake to sick babies.

It's time for the nightly ritual. "Sara," I query, "tell me some good things about today."

"Oh Mama," she laughs. "We could be up all night."

Friday morning Sara suffers after-birthday blahs. "Shape up, Sissy-girl," I order, rubbing her feet.

"I'm cranky because the back of my mouth is sore from

cutting these nine-year-old molars."

"Oh-oh. Let me look. You must have mouth sores."

She clenches her teeth and mutters, "molars."

"Well, you'd better tell Dr. J. about them at rounds, or else I will," I threaten. "There's no such thing as nine-year-old molars."

Dr. Johnson and the B-3 interns mask and clump into our room. I love to watch them pilfer Sara's drawings, study the autographs on the Benefit Dance poster, and paw through her newest negligées draped over the IV pole. Dr. Sarah always pets a fleecy lamb, while Dr. Pearson's eyes never leave Sara's face.

"For a gal with no white count you look pretty chipper. How you feeling, sweetheart?"

"Perfect," she says, shifty-eyeing her mama. I dip my head, purse my lips, lift my brows. "Except for these darn nine-year-old molars coming in."

"I told her there's no such thing," I say, with a condescending isn't-she-cute titter. "Mouth sores are more like it."

"Remember," Sara straight-eyes Dr. Johnson, "I told you, I'm never going to get mouth sores."

"Let me take a peek." Sara opens wide as Dr. J. solemnly studies her mouth, then announces, "Sure enough, it looks pretty sore where those nine-year-old molars are coming in. Use that Nystatin regularly, Sara. It'll ease the discomfort."

I look for a wink from the interns, but they are as deadpan as their leader. Sara smugs, "Three times a day. I'll let you know when they pop through."

"Absolutely." Dr. J. and his brood troop out fast.

"Well, I guess I learned something today, Sara," I say.

"Good for you, Mama."

I coffee with Gayle in the hallway. She is excited and scared. Erin's new marrow has grafted and her counts are high enough to leave the hospital. The Jameses will all move into the 47th Street house and Erin will be monitored through daily clinic visits. I hug Gayle, and hope our family follows close behind. "We'll still visit every day," Gayle says, and I remind her we are only three blocks apart.

Gayle and I settle into our favorite game, What Kind of Car Does Doctor So-and-So Drive, with variations, until Sara yells that Grandma's on the phone.

Mom says they'll be over tomorrow to see our new house and to deliver Sara's handmade birthday gift. "Can't wait," I say. "Things are going great."

Walt comes to stay with Sara today, and I lie in the sun on 20th Street while Andy naps in his bedroom. The steamy heat and guilt-free feeling is heady stuff. I'm giddy when I arrive back at the hospital to dress for Nurse Nancy's 7:00 p.m. wedding ceremony.

Walt and I leave Sara in Andy's care, laughing at her parting words, "Memorize everything, Mama. Memorize."

Radiant Nancy descends a winding stairway on the arm of her father, like an angel from heaven. She joins Don at the altar, and when Walt sneaks my hand in his, we are once again, just for a bit, crazy, carefree in love.

At the champagne reception, Nancy swooshes in, scans the crowd, and floats our way. "Oh, I'm so glad you're here," she says. "I want Sara to have this." And she pulls the rosebud center from her bridal bouquet. "She loves roses, you know."

"Right," I say. "Be happy, Nancy. Don't cry." And Walt and I dump our drinks and head for the hospital.

We report in detail to Sara and the B-3 staff. The ethereal bride, the star-struck groom, and who was with whom. Then Walt trundles Andy, the bombed-out babysitter, home.

Sara's bridal Barbie Doll descends the bed rails well into the night. Clutching an oversized rosebud bouquet.

Sunday afternoon, Walt, Andy and Dad run errands while Mom and I admire Sara. Mom has sewn a floor-length *Little House on the Prairie* dress with matching bonnet, and Sara twirls, a turn-of-the-century doll-baby.

"Oh, thank you, Grandma," she squeals. "Now I don't even feel too sad about missing Annie and the Orphans today."

"Who?" slightly out-of-it Grandma inquires.

"Little Orphan Annie from the Broadway musical is performing in the rec-room today," I explain. "We'll go hear her and tell Sara all about it. Rec-room Patty is recording it too."

We leave Sara primping, and squeeze into the packed playroom. Before us sparkles a bunch of beautiful nine- and ten-year-old girls, smiling and waving to wheelchaired, banana-carted, real sick kids.

"I don't know if I can take this," whispers Mama, and I just shake my head, afraid to talk.

With a razzmatazz piano intro, Annie and the orphans belt out, "You're Never Fully Dressed Without a Smile," and with the bang-up finish, the whole room cheers. Fully dressed.

While the orphans settle behind her, shiny-eyed Annie stands alone, with her hands clasped in front of her, takes a big breath and lays it on:

> The sun'll come out, tomorrow,
> Bet your bottom dollar, that tomorrow
> There'll be sun.
> Just thinkin' about tomorrow
> Clears away the cobwebs and the sorrow
> Til there's none.
> When I'm stuck with a day
> That's grey and lonely,
> I just stick out my chin,
> And grin and say, Oh
> The sun'll come out tomorrow
> So you gotta hang on til tomorrow
> Come what may.
> Tomorrow, tomorrow,
> I love ya, tomorrow
> You're always a day away.

I accidentally look at rec-room Patty. Our eyes bump, then make a fast getaway. Mama and I link arms and join the wild applauding audience of true believers.

"Was it wonderful?" Sara asks.

"Fantastic," I report. "We'll buy the tape and you can hear it over and over again."

There's a soft knock on our door, and rec-room Patty grins through the glass, motioning us to the cracked-open door.

"Hi, Sara," shouts a gaggle of little girls. Annie leads the orphans in a stirring rendition of "Happy Birthday To You," and Sara says, "You sure sing better than my doctors . . . but don't tell them I said so."

"I love your dress, Sara."

"Your room is neat, Sara."

"You sure must have a ton of friends, Sara."

"Who made your doll, Sara?"

"That blanket is beautiful, Sara."

"Here's an autographed program, Sara. Please get well soon," says Annie.

Sara pulls her bonnet close and waves goodbye through the window. Smiling a sweet sad smile.

A little before six, Grandma and Grandpa love Sara goodbye. She pouts and wails, "Who's going to stay with me tonight? Mom and Dad and Andy are going out to dinner with the Borgstroms, and you're going home. And I'll be all alone."

"Knock it off, Sissy," Walt says. "Mama will be back here by eight." We settle her with pens, paper, TV and kisses, then drive to the Conquistador.

Eye-watering *chimichangas* fail to melt the frozen memory of Sara's forsaken little face as she clutched my sleeve and pleaded, "Hurry back, Mama." And I am relieved when dinner's over and my boys drop me off at the main entrance to COH. While I wait for the elevator, I am the nun in the children's book, *Madeline*. "In the middle of the night, Miss Clavel turned on the light and said, 'Something is not right!'"

B-3 is deserted. The ward clerk is gone. The nurses' station is empty. And the patients' doors are shut, shades drawn. There is a piercing howl coming from the end of the corridor. A new admit in 312, restrained by two aides, a nurse and grey-faced parents, flails desperately to avoid Dr. Pearson and his IV needle. Leaning over the little boy's legs, Adrian says, "Sara needs you bad."

Sara has lost it all. My daughter rages at the window on her door, beating her head, sobbing, shaking, clawing. I race in without masking, grab her onto my lap, and rock back and forth, back and forth. "It's all so sad," she cries over and over and over again, while I rock harder, harder, harder. Finally she nestles into rhythmic hitches, and I kiss her bald head and steamy cheeks.

"What happened tonight, Sissy?" I breathe into her ear.

"It's that new kid," she whispers. "He's screaming now, but it's just the beginning. He doesn't know what he's in for. And it's all so sad."

"He's not your worry, Sara. Besides, they haven't even diagnosed him yet."

"He's got it, Mama. He has bruises all over. I know he's got it."

I hug her harder and promise, "I won't leave you again, Sara. It's getting too hard to be trapped in here alone, isn't it?"

She snuggles. "Thank you, Mama. I love you so much." Then she straightens and backs off. "Get a mask on and wash those hands, you rascal. Then go fix us a cup of peppermint tea."

"Are you sure you won't beat the door down if I walk out of here again?" I joke.

"You're not funny," she frowns, wearing her hospital face.

After tea and talk, Sara passes out, exhausted. I wait my turn for the shower. "What a night!" Adrian collapses. "It took all of us to start that IV, then Sara went bolos and we couldn't help her. I'm really sorry."

"I understand," I nod. "I think she's just been cooped up too long. It's getting to her. I hope her counts start coming up soon."

"They will," Adrian promises, patting my hand.

After my shower, I call Walt and describe the evening.

"We can't leave her alone any more," he agrees. "Tonight makes you know it's been worse for her than she's let on, doesn't it?"

"Yeah," I whisper. "But she's getting well."

"Right," Walt says. "We'll be up for breakfast in the morning. Get some sleep."

Just before I zee off, Barb Jacobs calls and says Jill wants to see Sara tomorrow. Is it OK?

Jill, born one month before Sara. Jill, Walt's practice run. Barb came down from her mountain to labor at our house early that morning, July 6, while Ed pumped gas up the street. His summer job.

When Barb called O.B. and said, "Well, I guess they're a minute or two apart," Walt collapsed in the rocking chair and gawked at the big-bellied time bomb. Barb hung up and announced, "It's time to go now. Will you take me to Ed, Walt?"

"Just as soon as I shave and shower," Walt answered.

"Is that really necessary? It's just three blocks to the gas station," Barb smirked.

"Right. Right. I think you're right," Walt agreed, and charged the car, eager to be rid of this hot potato.

A month later Sara arrived and we resumed our Friday-night pinochle parties, while the godsisters lay side by side, becoming best friends.

At terrible two, Jill ripped into Ed's cigarettes and Sara tattled, "Jill 'moked."

At trusting three, hand in hand, the friends tiptoed into the pasture to "pet the bull" . . . and moseyed into a ripe drainfield. Barb and I plucked our blue-jeaned babies from the knee-deep gunk and hosed them down. Sara's twelve-buck tennis shoes were missing, but no one volunteered to retrieve them.

At fun-loving four, Jill said, "Wanna play monsta?" And costumed in old prom dresses, Brides of Frankenstein, they sat in a dark closet and whispered God knows what.

The fantastic fives trundled off to kindergarten, sharing lunch boxes, boyfriends and whirling walks home. They grew at the same rate, always within a pound and an inch of each other. Barb, Ed, Walt and I marveled at the best buddies. Perfect complements.

Jill wants to see Sara tomorrow. "Please hurry," I answer.

When the Jacobses arrive outside her door, Sara flurries into action, lining up Nancy Drew books, arranging lotions and potions, dumping Barbie and her entourage all over the hide-a-bed.

I beg Nurse Marshall to let Jill mask and sit with Sara for a while. Marshall says, "That would be the best medicine of all." We leave the girls cross-legged on the bed, with the emesis pan as Barbie's kidney-shaped swimming pool, a Kleenex-box Barbie bed and the intercom call button in Sara's hot little hand.

"Whatever you want, Jill. Just let me know and I'll order it up."

"Last of the big-time spenders," Marshall says. "I'll keep an eye on them. Have a good lunch."

We go to the Burgermaster, then cruise University Village. When we return, it's like old times.

"Does Jill have to go home now? She just got here."

"Barbie just started her honeymoon."

"Why don't you have one more cup of coffee."

Jill's mom says that Sara will be home soon, and then they can play all day long. But for now, the ferryboat waits. The best friends exchange "It's no fair" frowns, and Sara says, "Don't forget your doughnut and your grapes and your yogurt and your root beer," and Jill packs them up.

"Where did you get all that garbage?" Ed gasps.

"Sara ordered it up for me, of course."

"I get whatever I want, you know," Sara brags.

"Yeah, and it'll be a big tumble back to earth when we blow this joint, Sissy, old girl," I warn.

She laughs, tucking Fritos into Jill's pocket, hugging a final farewell.

While Sara sleeps, I sneak out to sit with Marshall. "It was wonderful," she says. "Every few minutes Sara buzzed the desk with a gourmet request." The staff got a chuckle out of Sara's power trip. But best of all, says Marshall, was the little bald girl, modeling Barbie's bridal veil, sporting Frito fangs, while her best friend lay laughing beside her on the bed. "A treasure," Marshall says. "My treasure."

"By the way," she adds, "Sara's counts started up today. Dr. Johnson will see you in the morning."

But instead, he sends the message with Dr. Niebrugge, a hematology fellow taking Dr. Balis's place. If Sara's white count continues up, we move to 20th Street tomorrow.

It takes forever for the lab work to get done Wednesday, August 13, and we hang in limbo. "Do we pack up or not?" I fuss.

Dr. Niebrugge says, "Sure. You can always unpack."

Around three, Marshall says counts are in, and even

though Sara's are lower than they were yesterday, we can check out today.

Walt, Sara and Andy fly into action, but I panic. "I don't get it, Marshall. Why doesn't she still need isolation? How can they send her out with no defenses? It just doesn't make sense."

"I'll ask Dan to come talk to you," she soothes.

Dr. Niebrugge sits on his haunches, leaning against the wall, and chuckles, "What's with you, Carol? You can't wait to leave us, but when we give you the green light, you beg to stay."

"I'm hardly begging to stay," I flare. "Just explain why she couldn't even leave her room yesterday, and with her counts even lower today, you're sending her out of the entire hospital."

"You know our method of counting cells is far from perfect. We know she's got a graft. We know she feels good. We know her counts will continue up. Take it and run. We'll see her in clinic every day. Satisfied?"

"I want to see Dr. Johnson," I huff.

"I'll let him know," Dan Niebrugge sighs. And I wish he weren't so nice.

Dr. J. puts his arm around me and says he understands my confusion, for sure. But he feels the psychological advantages of a release outweigh the medical risks. "I'm a phone call away," he promises, giving me his home number. "Just keep her out of crowds and sunshine. Enjoy being a family again. Feel better?"

"I do," I smile. "Thanks."

Our release papers are ready, and as we walk away from B-3, Sara checks back over her shoulder. "I'm a little sad," she mumbles. "I'll probably never live here again."

"And that makes you *sad*?" Walt is incredulous.

"We had some good times here. Didn't we, Mama?"

We sign the discharge at the cashier's desk and I tuck our

copy into safekeeping for Sara's scrapbook. Someone has scrawled across the officious form, "Good Luck, Sara!"

Sara seemed strong and in charge, cocooned in 313, but climbing the steps on 20th Street, she struggles, weak and vulnerable. Walt and I watch from the driveway as Andy bounds to the porch, then backtracks and takes his sister's hand.

After dinner, Andy shares the house's nooks and crannies with Sara. They want to sleep together, but wary of infection, we tuck Andy onto a cot in the dining room.

While Walt unloads the car, I set up the H.A. line supplies on the dresser in our bedroom, and unpack.

When we kiss our sleeping kids one more time tonight, our clothes hang in the closets, our quilts cover the beds, our toys clutter the living-room floor. Sara snores through our goodnight affections, but Andy stirs, scrunches into his kitty blanket and says, "It's good to be four again."

The kids rustle out early in the morning, Legos snap and cartoons blare. Andy's hungry and Sara wants her line flushed. While Walt makes pancakes, I clean and dress Sara's H.A. site, then flush and lock her line. She eyeballs, then critiques my every move. And when we're finished I'm a wreck and Sara's exhausted.

"We must have a heart-to-heart, Sissy-girl," I say. "The H.A. nurses wouldn't have let me bring you home if they didn't think I could handle your line. I certainly don't mind you helping me, but I resent the fact that you treat me like I'm trying to do you in. Give me a break."

"Well," she sulks, "I'd rather do it myself."

"Well, you can't," I bristle.

"Can I do the clamps at least?" she bargains.

"A deal," I agree. And arm in arm we head for Dad's pancakes.

Sara's counts skyrocket this week. We go daily to the clinic for blood work, physical exam and a once-over with Dr. Johnson. He's excited to hear that Sara and her brother play the days away, enjoying our shaded porch and a daily romp in the park nearby. He's ecstatic when we report she can still hand-over-hand the crossbars, pump a swing halfway to heaven, and spin her brother on the merry-go-round. "Supah, just supah," he laughs. "Take a couple days off. We won't need to see Sara again until Monday."

Saturday, Sara and Andy play postman with the mail slot in our front door. Walt and I pluck messages off the carpet all day.

But Sara turns cranky in the afternoon, won't go to the park, refuses dinner, and goes to bed early.

"Don't worry," says Walt. "It's been a long week. She's just tired."

"I know," I affirm. "And this is about the time transplants turn listless and drowsy from the radiation."

Still, we lay tense, wrapped up scared tonight.

Sunday, Sara snarls at Andy, "Get out of my room. I want privacy." When he backs off angry and hurt, Walt grabs him for a wrestle, then the boys dig into the Lego Space Station.

I lie with Sara on the living-room couch, rubbing the back she turns my way. "I think you owe your brother an apology, Sissy. What do you think?"

"I think my hands itch bad, Mama," she sobs. "And the bottoms of my feet, too." I close my eyes, light-headed, looseboweled. Heartsick.

"Let me see, Sissy," I coax. She turns over, tight-fisted. I pry her hands open and study the red-rashed palms.

"I got G.V.H.," she whispers.

"A little bit of it," I answer. I am amazed at the nonchalance in my voice—and so is Sara.

"Are you scared?"

"I am," I admit. "But remember, Dr. J. likes to see a little G.V.H. rash. He says kids who show a little rash don't relapse as often. That new marrow is diggin' in there to stay. I'm going to call now, and see what we need to do. OK?"

She nods and tightens into a little knot. Walt follows me to the phone and we hold each other tight before I dial the hospital and ask for the hematologist on call.

"Yes, I know about Sara," he says. "I'm going to call Len Johnson and see how to proceed. I'll get right back to you." When we hang up, Walt and I sag into the corner. Rag dolls.

I snatch the phone in half a ring. "Hello?" I demand.

"Hi. Dr. Johnson wants to start Sara on Prednisone. It's a steroid that is sometimes helpful with G.V.H."

"Yeah. I know all that. What about the itching? It's really bothering her."

"We'll prescribe Benadryl for that. Can you pick it up at the hospital pharmacy right away?"

"My husband will be right over."

"OK. Dr. Johnson says he'll see you in Clinic tomorrow, and feel free to call him at home if you have any questions tonight.

While Walt makes the medicine run, I bed down Andy, then rub Sara's itchy feet.

"You know, Erin has quite a rash now, too. You girls will

be twins in Clinic tomorrow. I guess the Prednisone is really helping her. She doesn't even need Benadryl any more.''

Sara nods, twitches a little smile, and curls into herself.

After medication, she sleeps still, sedated, on her back with the streetlight illuminating her worried little face. Walt thinks her cheeks look blotchy and I cry into his chest.

Gayle James and I hold hands in Clinic while Sara and Erin have blood drawn. "I just know Erin will never smile again,'' the little mama worries. "Somebody told me that God never gives you anything you can't handle, Carol. But I know we can't handle any more of this." We talk of the strains cancer puts on finances, friendships and marriages, then shrug and acknowledge we have no choice but to muddle on the best we can.

"I'll call tonight," I promise as Sara and I shuffle into an exam room.

"How ya doin', sweetheart?" Dr. Johnson smiles, with eyes only for Sara. "Rosy cheeks," he says, rubbing Sara's shoulders.

"Rosy hands and rosy feet, too," she volunteers, displaying her palms and wriggling her toes. "But not itchy any more."

"Well, your counts look good, Sara. We'll go with the Prednisone and look you over every day. Remember Lynsey Hunter? She had a little G.V.H. rash and she's home and doing supah now. You and Andy going to the park today?"

"Maybe. How's Nikki?"

Dr. J. leans against the window sill, hands clasped in front of him. "She's uncomfortable, Sara. We're moving her back into the hospital. She's having bladder problems and she and her family need some rest. I'll tell her you asked after her."

"And give her this." Sara pulls a homemade booklet titled, "Six Things To Do When You Are Blue," from her pink satin jacket pocket.

"Marvelous artwork, Sara," Dr. J. raves. "Nikki'll love it."

"I have more if she finishes that one." Sara climbs down from the exam table and walks into the hall to look at the photographs on the bulletin board.

"It's a waiting game, Carol," Dr. Johnson sighs. "We'll hope to contain it with the steroid, but be alert for more rash or diarrhea. We'll see you tomorrow." He scrapes up Sara's chart and backs slowly out the door.

I hover over Sara all week, examining her body morning and night, shrilling through the locked bathroom door, "Is everything OK?" And accusing Sara after every flush, "If you have even a trace of the scoots, I'd better know about it." When Sara snorts and slits her eyes, I add, "And I mean it, too."

Walt begs me to back off, and finally I can, on Thursday, when Dr. Johnson grins, "She's responding well to the Prednisone. Would you like to go home to Sequim this weekend?"

"You're kidding!" I say.

"She looks supah, Carol. The rash is contained. Her counts are good. I think we're home free."

"Did you hear that, Sissy? We're going home."

She smiles a thin dutiful little smile. "For how long?" she mutters.

"How about until Wednesday afternoon?" Dr. Johnson suggests.

Sara shrugs and nods.

"She's in shock," I explain. "And worried about how she's going to get all her new stuff into her little bedroom."

"School starts pretty soon. And I'm gonna go," Sara announces.

"We talked that one over. Remember? Not until after Christmas, Sara. It takes a while for that new marrow to really get rolling. And that leaves you open to all those school-kid germs. Besides, your mom says she's got a tutor all lined up for you."

"And I'll have hair by Christmas," she says, rubbing her new sprouted stubble.

"Supah hair, I'm sure," Dr. J. affirms.

We celebrate our great joy with phone calls home and Kidd Valley hamburgers. Sara picks at hers and says maybe she's too excited to eat. But she doesn't seem excited. And she conks out early on the couch.

"She'll be so much better at home," Walt says, packing her into her room.

"In her own bed," I add.

I hear the toilet flush in the night and I bolt up and wait for Sara outside the bathroom door. "I only peed," she says. "Go back to bed and think about being home free."

"Maybe we'll leave here tomorrow, Sissy. What difference would one day make?"

"He said we could go Saturday, Mama. Not Friday."

"Don't you want to go home, Sara?"

"Of course I do. But I'm a little nervous, you know."

"Yeah. Me too. But I keep thinking about the dog and the cats and our friends . . ."

"And my dollhouse," she dreams.

"I'll call Dr. J. in the morning and ask."

"I bet he'll say, 'Supah'," Sara chuckles, nuzzling into her pillow.

We pack up in the morning, and when I reach Dr. Johnson in Clinic and ask permission to fly the coop a day early, he says, "Supah, just supah." And before I hang up, we're halfway out the door.

We sing and joke all the way home, but when we pull up into our driveway, Walt can't find the house key, so he goes around back to enter through the utility porch. When he flings open the front door, he's foaming at the mouth and smoking at the ears. "That damn dog. That goddamn dog scratched right through the goddamn back door. That's it! We're gonna get rid of that goddamn dog!"

Muffin, the big black hangdog, skulks guilty, wood splinters hanging from her chops. "Get outta here!" Walt roars, and she lowtails it into the back yard.

The kids run wailing to their rooms. "Dad's going to sell our dog!"

And I pounce. "Well, this is a joyous homecoming. Here we are home together, folks, for the first time in six weeks, and you're insane over a goddamn dumb door. May I suggest you get your act together and straighten out this mess?"

"I'm sorry, I'm sorry," Walt shouts. "I'm just so tight I'm ready to snap."

We stand in our living room glaring, tight-lipped, hating. "It's never going to go away," I whisper. "We're going to be scared the rest of our lives."

We hold each other tight, and Walt says, "We just need a good night's sleep."

"In our own bed," I reply.

Our answer for everything.

Sara and Andy stand wide-eyed in the hallway. "Well, at least we won't have to open the door to let the dog in any more," Walt laughs.

And the kids laugh, too.

"I think the door looks, 'supah, just supah'," Sara jokes in her best Dr. J. Australian accent.

We putter away the weekend. Walt patches the door, Andy swarms the neighborhood, I vacuum the house and Sara designs thank-you stationery. Kenny Rogers croons into our living room.

"We really know what the words to that one mean, don't we, Mom?" Sara shouts over the Hoover.

"What? I can't hear you," I frown, clicking the switch to OFF.

"This song, Mama. We know all about it." And I sit down and listen.

> Love lifted me, love lifted me,
> When nothing else would do,
> You know, love lifted me.
>
> Love lifted me, love lifted me,
> When I was down and out,
> You know, love lifted me.

"For sure, Sara," I whisper. "And your drawing is perfect."

Sara has penned two little girls exchanging flowers in a rose garden, while a dog and cat smile nearby. She titles it, "Friends Are the Flowers in the Garden of Life."

"Thanks," she smiles, rubbing her chest, and I notice the rash has crept down her body and up her arms.

Monday, I take Andy to the pediatrician for his kindergarten check up and booster shots. Sara stays with Grandma to visit and bake cookies. She's cranky, restless, fiery-cheeked, and I tell Mom I'm worried about her.

"She probably senses you're kind of edgy, honey," Mom assures me. "Her rash seems a little brighter, but I think she's OK."

Andy passes his physical with flying colors and fails to flinch when he's injected. "Sara's great," we brag to the doctors. "Some G.V.H., but Dr. Johnson thinks we're home free."

"It's just a miracle," raves a receptionist.

"The answer to a lot of prayers," adds her cohort.

When we return to Grandma's house, Sara lies hunched on the couch, staring out the big windows at Grandpa's rose garden. Grandma looks hot and bothered. "She doesn't have much zip," Mom confides. "But she ate two bran muffins and wanted a third. She loves to look at the roses."

"I wish we had some at our house." Sara says.

"We'll plant some this fall, Sissy. Something to do while you're home from school," I promise.

She smiles, tired.

Monday night Sara won't eat or drink. Her tummy's a little queasy, she says. Probably those muffins. Grandma agrees. "Those darned things'll do it every time."

On Tuesday afternoon, Sara vomits into the sink. By evening, dry heaves convulse her red-rashed body.

I call COH and talk to Dan Niebrugge. "She has an appointment tomorrow afternoon, but would you be more comfortable bringing her over tonight?" he asks. Walt and I confer and decide to leave early in the morning. Grandma and Grandpa will pick up Andy. Dr. Dan says call any time during the night and we can talk. I take him up on the offer, and spend much of Tuesday's wee hours sobbing my worries into the phone while Walt lies beside Sara.

She sleeps most of the way to Seattle, wrapped in her quilt, and holding a pan.

Walt delivers us to the sixth-floor Clinic entrance, and when I help Sara from the car, she collapses and says she can't walk. I haul a wheelchair to the curb, we load her up, and in the morning sunlight, Sara is a slumped-over, shriveled-up shell. Walt parks the car, and I wheel Sara into the hospital, her head in her hands, my teeth slicing my lips.

And when we roll into Hematology, I give Sara over and fall to pieces in the arms of Irene, the Clinic nurse.

They lay Sara in a treatment room and Dr. Johnson tells Walt and me that he will perform the scheduled bone-marrow aspiration. "It might give us some answers."

Sara is dehydrated and the nurses hook her up to fluids. "It looks as though the G.V.H. has internalized," Dr. Johnson says. "And the gut is involved. But first things first. We'll get the aspiration out of the way, settle her onto B-3 and go from there."

While Len Johnson prepares Sara for the bone-marrow aspiration, he coos soft and low, "Have ya been worryin' about this poke, sweetheart? Maybe your tummy just has a bad case of nerves, Sara. We'll get this out of the way, darlin', and you might perk right up."

She searches his face, closes her bloodshot eyes, and nods. The procedure, performed by the expert, is over before we have time to work up our usual tears. And Sara whispers, "If I ever have to have another bone-marrow, will you do it, Dr. J.?"

"It's a promise," he replies, touching her cheek with the

backs of his fingers.

Sara slumps into a wheelchair, elbows on knees, patchy face resting on measled fingers.

The floor is quiet, shadowed, breath-bated. Nancy going off duty, Jeannette coming on. "Hi, Nancy," Sara apologizes.

And Nancy stiffens, "Hi, kiddo."

"Will you pull the shades, Nancy? I want to be all alone in the dark."

"Sure, Sara. You're all hooked up. Here's the call button pinned to your sheet. Rest and I'll see you in the morning." Nancy hurries out the door.

"You leave, too," Sara orders, and Walt and I obey. While Walt stares at the basketball court outside the living-room window, I sit beside Nancy on a plastic couch.

"Oh, God. She looks like a heme kid," Nancy moans. "Up until today, even bald and skinny, she was so beautiful. But now. Oh, God. She looks like a heme kid."

"I know," I sob. "I'm afraid she's thrown it out. And I don't have anything to pump back into her."

"But you will," Walt threatens. "We all will."

Jeannette joins us, says Sara's asleep, and asks if we need anything.

"I need to know how Nikki's doing," I answer. "Is she still in Intensive Care?"

Jeannette and Nancy look at each other, and Jeannette says, "I guess they didn't tell you in Clinic, Carol. Nikki died last night."

I go to Walt at the window and we rock together, wailing

big and loud for Nikki. And for ourselves.

Sara's call-light flashes orange and we pick up our pieces and follow Jeannette into 315. Sara vomits into a towel, and the flecks of blood frighten her. "It's OK, Sara," Jeannette says "Your tummy's really irritated, so there's a little bleeding. It's OK, Sara."

Sara lies back and asks for water. "Swish, but don't swallow," Jeannette says. "We don't want anything to go down for a while."

"Rub my feet, Mama," Sara says. "They're itchy."

"Sure," I say. "I'll use Baby Magic."

Walt takes one foot and I take the other, and while we massage, Sara asks, as I knew she'd ask, "How's Nikki doing, Mama?"

"Sissy," I begin. "You remember that Nikki came down with pneumonia a few days ago? Well, her body was too tired to fight any more. Nikki died last night."

"No, no." Sara gags, drawing her feet away from us, pulling her quilt over her face. I lay my arm across Sara, but she hisses, "go away and leave me alone."

Walt takes my hand and we pace outside Sara's door. Walt says he's got to get out for a while. He'll bring back some coffee. And while I sit wondering if I'll ever see the Clines again, a familiar voice booms, "Little sister, God love ya, I'm so sorry y'all had to come back to this."

I stand up to hug Roger Cline and cry into his belly while he comforts me. *He* comforts *me*! "Woman," he says, "Nikki's at peace. Why, I saw her this mornin' while I slept. She was sittin' on the lap of sweet Jesus. Laughin'. She had long blonde hair. And she was laughin'. Oh, I'm wounded, girl. It's a fresh cut and it stings. But it'll heal. And one of these days I'll be left with just a scar. Just a memory of this horrible pain. And Nikki? She's got it all now. She's got Paradise.''

I pull away from Roger Cline, wiping my nose on my sleeve.

"Carol," he whispers, his eyes flashing like sunlight on bottlecaps. "Just before Nikki left us, the nurse called me into the room to point out this white pigeon that'd been a-sittin' on the ledge outside the window all night long. Strange, she says. Not so strange, I say. And I tell her about our B-3 birds. And girl, when Nikki left, so did that pigeon. Hallelujah! She has been released!''

He grabs hold for one more bear hug. And I feel sucked in. Against my will.

"May I see my beautiful Sara? To tell her goodbye. We're all takin' off tomorrow after we make arrangements to fly Nikki's body home.''

"Sure," I answer. "Sara knows about Nikki. She's angry and scared.''

Roger tiptoes into the darkened room, and Sara's wise, rheumy little eyes draw him close. "I'm so sad," she offers.

"I know you are, my darlin'. But now you've got a job to do. You're gonna fight. And you're gonna get up and walk out of here. You're gonna run and skip and dance. For Nikki. I love you, Sara.''

And she nods and smiles. But does not cry.

When Roger Cline leaves, Sara asks for pens and stationery. And to be left alone again.

While she writes, Walt and I meet with Dr. Johnson in the living room. The marrow looks pretty good, he says. Just a few of the type of cells they see in severe G.V.H. "What I want to do, Walt and Carol, is to give Sara's gut a complete rest. We'll support her with hyperalimentation through the line, increase the Prednisone, and wait it out.'' He explains that Sara's gut is peeling, just like her skin, and that our hope is that the underlying new tissue will be healthy. "Remember this," he says. "If she makes it through this, we can almost guarantee there will be no relapse, ever.''

"I'm so worried about her spirit,'' I say. "She doesn't seem to have any fight left. She thinks she's going down the same road as Nikki Cline. And sometimes I'm afraid she might be right.''

"Nikki and Sara are completely different cases,'' Dr. Johnson says firmly. "Nikki was transplanted in relapse, and suffered immediate G.V.H. The graft was never good. Sara was transplanted in remission and has a good functioning graft. I'm going to talk to Sara now, and tell her exactly what I told you.''

Len Johnson walks in and settles beside Sara on the bed. He relays the game plan, talks about Nikki, and promises never to lie. "If ever I think you're losing the battle, Sara, I'll tell you. But for now, I want you to rest and concentrate on growing new healthy skin, inside and out.''

Sara lies hypnotized by the gentle man beside her. "I will,'' she whispers. "Will you give this to the Clines?'' She hands Dr. J. an envelope crayoned with bright balloons and sealed with a happy-face sticker.

Sara has penned a message on the flap, "Keep your chin up!''

Between bouts of bloody diarrhea and red-streaked vomiting, Sara lies perfectly still. Two days pass, and the constant testing of her output, the adjusting and readjusting of nutrients in the H.A. fluid, the careful monitoring of her vital signs, become routine. The way we live now.

Still, Sara lies limp, listless. Worried. Together with our physicians and Patti, the family therapist, we make a difficult decision. Sara needs to believe again that she's getting well. Perhaps the ever-present Daddy tells her that a crisis must be imminent. We tell Sara today that because her condition is stable, Daddy's going home to teach school and start Andy off to kindergarten. It will be like old times. We'll all be together on the weekends. Sara smiles agreement, says, "That's best for Andy. I love you, Daddy."

As part of our "back to normal" scheme, I tell Sara she must crawl out of COH night shirts and back into her own pretty pj's. Before Walt heads home, I whip down to the Village and buy Sara a lace-trimmed, hooded, red velour robe. We zip her into it, and Walt kisses his big babydoll goodbye.

Now we wait for our tough-love to work. The teenage boy across the hall aids and abets our cause.

He flexes up and down the floor, pumping iron, swaggering near, acutely aware of our curiosity. Proud of it. Scorning it. Lean, mean, sixteen. Joe.

Sara lies on her right side, counting the passes Joe makes by her room. Maybe she has laid down to die. But Joe is bringing her back to us.

Sara dubs the six-foot, two-inch teenager Big Joe, and it sticks. Big Joe is up for total body radiation in the morning, in preparation for his bone-marrow transplant. He attained a first-round remission, is physically strong, and has a perfectly matched sibling donor. They say he's a lucky one.

Big Joe doesn't read it that way. The big beautiful body-gone-bad betrays him. And with adolescent vengeance, he punishes it. The world that is supposed to await him, rebuffs him. And the white letters on his red cap snarl, "Fuck off."

After lifting weights most of the afternoon, Big Joe checks out on pass for the evening. One last bash before his transplant. As he rumbles out the door, red cap jaunty on his bald head, the nurses wager on whether he'll bother to return. I don't wait up for him, but Sara does.

Curled onto a couch, she hovers by the nurses' station, playing hangman with Catnip Karen. Joe stumbles in near four in the morning, weary, bleary. Stoned. He slumps in a chair across from the nine-year-old, peely-skinned granny, wrapped in her flannel quilt. Joe stares at Sara, struggling to focus, obscene hat askew.

"Big Joe," she says, quiet but firm, "I think your hat is extremely rude."

The nurses and aides take it in, wide-eyed. In the weeks Joe has worn The Hat, no one has challenged it. No one has even mentioned it.

To Joe, anyway.

The Hat has been the subject of countless conversations, but a definitive approach has not yet been worked out. No one has considered the direct route. Until now. The cowpokes circle the corral, and shuffle in for the showdown.

Joe's eyes blink, clear, then sparkle. "Do you think so, Sara? Do you really think so?" With a quick dip of her shiny head she affirms it. Joe smiles a tiny smile, removes his hat and shrugs off to bed. Sara dozes in the hallway after Karen promises to wake her for Joe's departure in four hours.

And when the ambulance attendants roll the Thorazined

big boy past his self-appointed guardian angel, she whispers words of widsom, "If you can throw up without the nurses having to come in to help you, it'll go faster. They won't have to turn off the radiation. When you feel cold, just remember, they keep it that way so you might feel less sick to your stomach. Good luck, Big Joe."

As the stretcher whisks onto the elevator, Sara sobs, "It's so sad. It's all so sad."

In the days that follow, Joe holes up, shades drawn, food uneaten, intimidating staff, insulting friends, offending family, until he is left alone.

Sara eavesdrops on the nurses' concern, and takes a few matters into her own hands. She sends a poster across the hall: a basset in the bathtub, captioned, "Was today really necessary?"

"Maybe he'll laugh," she says.

She orders me to buy Joe a Kidd Valley hamburger, because the nurses say teenagers really like them.

"But Sara," I complain, "that drive-in is five miles away."

"Tell Sue you need a ride," she commands. And I do it. We ship the burger across the hall, but Joe doesn't eat it. "That's OK," says Sara. "Sometimes it helps just to look at good food."

Each morning we raise Sara's shades, even though she'd rather hide in the dark. She decides that what's good for the goose is good for the gander. "Tell Joe he'll feel a little better if he looks outside for a while every day." And the next day one curtain lifts, and we wave to Joe swirled in marijuana smoke, used to fight his nausea.

"Too bad he hasn't learned to think it away," says Sara into her pillow.

Each night this week I call Walt from the lobby phone and reel off our ups and downs.

"The diarrhea's bad, but not so bloody."

"She listens to 'Tomorrow' on the 'Annie' tape all day long."

"She asked to watch 'Little House on the Prairie' tonight."

"Her days and her nights are turned around. I feel like a zombie."

Sara loves wee-hour banana-cart cruises. Between dates with the potty-pan, she wakens me to walk her around the deserted darkened corridors. She loves the sixth-floor waiting-room window with its view of the sparkling Seattle skyline.

"If that aide on four calls me 'Little Miss America' one more time, I might have to get rude. . . ."

"Nobody really knows how many stars there are in the sky. Where do they all come from? Too many to count."

"I love to listen to Andy sing those kindergarten songs. He's so cute. But you better be careful, Mama, not to let him get away with things. . . ."

FIVE

D R. Susan Marshall tiptoes in and smooths Sara's peeling cheeks. Our new intern is pretty, petite, perfectly pressed. A story-book doll.

Back from a predawn excursion, Sara lies on her right side, still, save for the slow rise-fall rise-fall of her quilt. My featherless baby bird, fallen from the nest, awaits rescue.

Sara squints open her bloodshot eyes, whispers, "Oh, Dr. Marshall," and smiles with caked, cracked lips.

"May I look you over before rounds, sweetheart?" Susan asks. And Sara smiles yes, rolls onto her back and gropes for the little green jeweled mirror Walt bought for her.

"I think that special soap is doing the job," Sara says of the gentle expensive magic potion Susan ordered from the pharmacy for Sara's crumbling skin. Sara peels away dead flakes and we cheer the birth of healthy new pink baby skin.

"Now let's go to work on your eyes, Sara. I've made an appointment in Eye Clinic. Think you and Mom can make it up there?''

"Yes," Sara nods.

I dress Sara in her red robe, bundle her onto the banana cart and trudge to the elevator. Sara pulls her hood up, hides the emesis bowl and the potty pan under the covers, and closes her eyes. "The lights are too bright," she complains.

The opthamologist suffers a bad case of artificial jollies. "Well, well, well. So this is Sara. Dr. Marshall told me all about you, Sara. Let's take a peek at your peepers."

Sara pinch-eyes the smiling young man, peels off her hood and vomits into blue plastic.

"Maybe you'd rather come back later when you feel better?" the doctor stammers.

"I feel like this all the time," Sara whispers, and eases into the exam chair.

The checkup is short, but thorough. Sara doesn't like her pupils dilated, and covers her face when we load her back onto the cart. While she rests, the opthamologist assures us that, though Sara's eyes are highly irritated by skin sloughing, no permanent damage is apparent. He prescribes a soothing eye cream and we promise to use it faithfully.

Back on B-3, Sara orders me into the hallway. "I need to be alone for a while," she says.

"Why do you always make me sit out there?" I ask. "I would be very quiet sitting beside your bed, reading my book."

"Oh, Mama, it's so sad. And I just need to be alone."

"OK, OK," I agree, kissing her cheek.

I am a lion at the library, stationed at my hallway post, guarding Sara's room. I read for a while, watch Sara sleep, then study Susan Marshall.

Gentle fingers tangled in curly black hair, brown eyes intense behind oversized frames, tiny figure perched properly at a little kid's table. Sara's savior-girl, surrounded by chicken-scratched tablet paper. She feels my stare, glances up, smiles, walks over and pulls up a wayward wheelchair.

"There's a new drug I'd like to try on Sara. I think it might help her nausea without making her so sleepy. If she tolerates it, no more Thorazine. I've just been figuring the proper dosage. What do you say?"

"We'll do whatever you think is best," I answer. Her shoulders sag and I'm immediately sorry for the burden we've handed her.

"I'll talk to Sara," she says, "and if she gives the OK, we'll give it a try."

When Susan explains the plan, Sara whispers, "I just don't want to zonk. Promise?"

"Promise," says Dr. Marshall. The new drug drips into Sara's line and we await miracles. "I'll check back this evening," Susan says. "Good luck."

"I love her, Mama."

"I know. I love her, too," I answer. And I worry about Susan Marshall. That we've dragged her in over her head.

Sara makes me sit in the hall while she rests, and I reluctantly comply. I watch her from the window and worry at what I see. Sara is restless and jerky. When I go in to talk to her she doesn't answer. She bolts up, eyes rolled into her head, neck stiff, arms rigid. "Look at me. Bring your eyes down," I command. "Stop that, Sara! Stop it right now!" I panic.

I yank the rails up on Sara's bed and race out to find a nurse. They are all congregated in Marty's room trying to start a new IV on the screaming, kicking, ten-year-old. I hate how she carries on over everything: baths, exercise, mouth care, IVs. "Shut up, you baby," I mutter. A new nurse on B-3 sees me standing outside Marty's door and comes out. "Something's very wrong with Sara," I report. "Her eyes are stuck open, her body's stiff and jerky. She needs help."

"Must be a reaction to the new drug. Be over in a sec." And she returns to Marty's bedside.

I am stunned into breaking an unwritten rule of B-3. I burst in on the doctors and nurses wrestling with Marty. "Sara needs help *right now!*" And when they look up, they are as sweaty and out of control as I am.

An intern nods dismissal to Miss New Nurse, and she follows me. Sara sits rigid behind the bars on her bed, just as I left her. The nurse looks her over, confers with an intern at the desk, and returns with Benadryl. Slowly Sara responds while I hold her. Her muscles relax and her eyes focus on me. "Oh, Mama," she cries. "I could hear you, but I couldn't answer. Like I was dead. I am so sad. I am so sad."

"Me too. Me too," I sob. And I hold her until she sleeps. Nurse Karen returns from break and untangles Sara and her out-of-control mother. Karen covers Sara while I cry at the end of the hall. When she joins me, she hugs me. And we rage together at the world crashing down all around us.

"A reaction like that is scary, but not dangerous," she promises. "We'll just go back to the Thorazine. If she'll let us." We laugh then, at what a brassy little broad Sara used to be. And how we'll know she's getting better when she starts giving orders again.

Late afternoon, put together again, I sit at my post watching Sara sleep. It's shift change and B-3 bustles. When the linen room door opens, I spy a curly head, face buried in a towel. Hematology fellow Diane Nugent comforts our tender little intern, and I love her even more. Susan Marshall cares enough to cry.

When she comes to me, she is warm but efficient. "I am so sorry about today," she begins. "I thought it was worth a try, but maybe I was wrong."

"Oh no," I interrupt. "You are the first one to understand how much Sara hates Thorazine. And you tried to help her. I know reactions are scary, but not dangerous."

Susan holds my hand and says, "Thank you."

Nancy pops in from the new B-2 assignment that she has requested. "Hi, Sara. Heard you had a really rough day today. Well, so did Lando. I'm on my way to visit him now."

Lando, Nancy's Dalmatian pup, suffers from parvovirus, a usually fatal disease.

"The vet's got him in Intensive Care now, on an IV, and I go just to sit with him. I feel so helpless." Tears track Nancy's cheeks. "You know?"

Sara studies Nancy's desperate face. Sara shuts her eyes. Turns away.

Nancy and I stand outside the room.

"I'm just so upset about my dog. I call about him every few hours. The vet says I should have him put to sleep, but I just can't." I pat her heaving shoulders. Nancy thinks she cries for her dog. But Nancy sorrows for Sara.

Sara's diarrhea is rampant and Dr. Johnson ups the Prednisone dose once more. The steroid increases thirst, and desperate Sara begs countless audiences with Dr. J. Three or four times a day Nurse Marshall calls the hematologist from Clinic, and Len Johnson faithfully treks down for negotiations.

"Just a swish?" Sara pleads.

"Sweetheart, just the presence of something in your mouth starts that digestive tract churning. And that irritates your super-delicate G.I. system. No swishes."

Sara orders me to line the windowsill with beverages—chocolate milk, apple juice, orange juice, pop—so that when Dr. J. gives the go-ahead, she'll be ready.

She begs me to drink my breakfast juice in her room, commanding, "Swig it down, Mama. Really swig it." When it's drained, she says, "Ahhh. That tasted so good."

"Don't make me do this, Sara," I plead. "You're just torturing yourself."

"Oh no, Mama. I feel much better after our juice."

"It's very strange," she says. "I never used to like grapefruit juice."

Sara haunts Dr. Johnson. She wants "only a swallow," and when she turns medical—"just five c.c.'s a day?"—he relents.

"We'll give it a go, darling. I'll arrange it with the nurses."

Nurse Marshall and rec-room Patty make a production of five c.c.'s of warm water. Patty packs in a miniature china tea set from the playroom, with four tiny cups. Wielding a syringe, Sara squirts the drops of water into each cup, and we girls play tea party.

Sara swirls the water, like fine wine, closes her eyes and sips. We all watch her, pretending not to, and look away as she wretches into her pan. "Darn it," she eases back onto her pillow. "Tell Dr. J. it was worth it anyway. And I can't wait for our party tomorrow."

Walt comes Friday after school. Sara kisses him, but is too weak for a hug. "Where's Andy?" she asks.

"He's coming over with Grandma and Grandpa in the morning," Walt answers.

"Good. I need to see him." She smiles and sleeps.

"You've got big puffs under your eyes," I tell Walt in the hallway. "You don't look so hot."

"Well, you're no peach yourself," he says.

He reads through Sara's flow sheets while I give him my evaluation. "She's no better but no worse. Everyone says it takes a while to come out of this. Sometimes months. It doesn't happen overnight."

"Right," he says.

The evening staff is jolly tonight; Walt's here. He fashions a cardboard box and aluminum-foil cover for Sara's IV stand, glues on eyes and a smile, then christens the 'droid R2-D2. Sara, Walt and the robot cruise B-3.

"Marvelous," someone raves.

"You should patent it," another says.

Walt grins and Sara closes her eyes.

Andy bursts in before noon on Saturday. I squeeze him hard, amazed at his strong, sturdy frame. "You're eating good, huh, Big Boy?"

"Of course," he squirms and bumps up to his sister. "Wanna play Barbies, Sissy? I'll even be a girl."

"No, Andy. And don't touch the bed. That hurts me."

Like a put-down playful puppy he nuzzles into my lap. "I thought you said she wanted to see me." I hug him tight.

"Come here, Andy," Sara whispers.

He shuffles back beside her, being careful not to bump the bed. "You can't play and you won't talk," he says. "Why do you even want me here?"

"I just needed to see your face," she replies. "I love your face."

He brightens and turns clown, making every goofy puss in his repertoire. Sara smiles, touches his fat cheek with a kiss and sleeps again.

Such a silent Sunday. Walt sits outside Sara's door reading the newspaper. Grandpa stares out the living-room window, arms folded across his chest. Andy colors on a clipboard, humming kindergarten tunes. Mom and I walk the hall.

Mama says, "Well, honey, her skin looks much better. And it's only natural she's weak. She's not eating."

I nod.

Mama says, "She said something kind of funny. She said, 'Keep a good eye on Andy.'"

I nod.

Mama says, "A strange thing to say, huh?"

I nod.

Wan September sunlight sifts into 315. Dust specks dance. And the family whispers goodbyes and I-love-yous.

"Do you want to have my Thumbkey, Sissy?" Andy asks, clutching his stuffed monkey close.

"Oh, no," she says. "You need to keep him, Big Boy."

Andy backs out the door with sad smile and tearful eyes. Sara blows him the tenderest little kiss. He catches it and plants it on his forehead.

Mom hugs me and says, "Remember, you're in everybody's prayers."

And I nod.

Monday morning a woman labeled, COH Medical Records stares at me in the elevator. "I've seen you around here a lot," she says. "Just what is your function, anyway?"

"I'm Sara's mother," I answer.

"Sara's a patient?" And she presses, "God, she's sure been here a long time. How long? What's she in for?"

"Four and a half months, on and off," I mumble. "She has cancer."

"Heav--yyy!"

When the elevator thumps down on three, my stomach lurches. Sick.

But by the time I get to the nurses' station, I'm laughing. Loud.

Day-shift nurses Barb and Buffy glance up, wondering, I'm sure, what I could possibly find funny. When I tell them the story, they laugh, too. Then Barb wraps her arm around my shoulders and says, "Nobody, *nobody* should have to put up with people like that."

Sara won't bathe this morning. She says she wants to rest up for "Little House on the Prairie" tonight. She sleeps between trips to the bathroom and I sit silent beside her. Willing my strength into the broken little body on the bed.

"Mama. Do you think Dr. Baker's baby will ever wear that Mickey Mouse shirt?"

"Of course I do, Sissy."

"Well, I don't think so, Mama. I feel so sad."

"I know you do, sweet girl," I croon, laying my head beside hers. Breathing in the strange sick smell of her.

When she sleeps I tiptoe away for a cup of coffee. Buffy motions me to the desk and Barb says, "Which hand?" They present me with Buffy's official COH I.D. badge, slightly altered. My name replaces Buffy's name and "Sara's Mother" is taped in over "R.N." A Mickey Mouse sticker covers Buffy's photograph.

"There," Barb says, pinning the card onto my T-shirt. "So you won't have to explain just-what-is-your-function-anyway, anymore."

"The red-haired coffee-shop cashier will love this," I say.

Over the months we've become friends, the red-haired coffee-shop cashier and I. She asks after Sara every morning as she rings up my breakfast. And one day she asks after me.

"You know," she says, counting out my change, "I was studying some literature last night, and it said parents of very sick children need a little TLC, too. I thought of you. So from now on, I'm going to ask how *you're* doing. And you can tell me about Sara if you feel like it. Deal?"

"Good deal," I answer, and we squeeze hands as she gives me my twenty-six cents.

In the evening I talk Sara through a bed change and sponge bath before "Little House on the Prairie."

"I have to lie on my left side to watch TV and I'm only comfortable on my right side," she says.

"No problem," Nurse Marshall says, ripping the fresh-made bed apart. "We'll just get a little tricky and put your head at the foot of the bed. I'll be sure and warn night shift so they don't stick a thermometer between your toes."

And Sara laughs. Not a big belly laugh. Just a little laugh. Her first laugh in three weeks.

She snoozes through her favorite TV show, but rouses for previews of next week's episode. "It's Almanzo and Laura's wedding coming up," she gasps. "What I've been waiting for all summer. I won't sleep next week, Mama. For sure."

I shower and buck up for another everlasting night. Sara wakes every hour to use the bathroom and I dread hearing her soft little apology, "Mama, I have to go again." I dread stumbling out of my warm bed, dread hoisting the too-weak-to-walk little girl, dread pushing the double-pumped IV pole into the toilet, dread hearing the spurt of tissue-flecked diarrhea spatter the potty pan, dread wiping the raw bony bottom.

"Oh, Mama, it's so hard for you to lift me," Sara whispers as I tuck her back into bed.

"Don't be silly, girl. It gives me an excuse to hug you." A lie. I hate hefting her. She hurts when the bed's bumped and our jostle into the bathroom is agony for her. She never complains, but soft groans give her away.

When I climb back under my quilt, Sara says, "I want to thank you, Mama, for sticking with me."

"Sissy, where else would I be? You're all that matters to

me right now. I love you with all my heart."

"I know that, Mama. And I love you."

Lying still, squeezing tears onto my pillow, I try once more to power my energy into Sara. To visualize her well and strong. When my last muscle finally sleeps, then comes the soft little apology, "Mama, I have to go again."

Sara asks for a tub bath Tuesday morning—and her red pajamas. She'd like to walk to the banana cart parked outside her room.

"Wonderful," crows Susan Marshall. "I'll walk with you."

It's Susan's last day on hematology service, before moving to Infant Intensive Care. Though she promises to visit every day, Sara remains drawn and silent over the imminent departure.

After lunch Suzanne peeps in. A dark-haired, ten-year-old sweetheart, Suzanne lost a leg to cancer a while back. When she comes for rehab, she always visits Sara.

"Hi," grins Suzanne. "Wanna play anything?"

"No. Wanna sit here for awhile?"

"Sure," she answers and plops into a chair.

No words, just loaded little smiles pass between the girls. And I'm an intruder on their silent sharing.

"I want some Orange Crush for my collection," says Sara.

"I'll buy some," I reply.

"I want to buy it myself."

"Oh honey, I don't think you can make it that far," I worry.

"I'll wear a Pamper," she whispers. "If you won't ever tell anyone."

When I tell Marshall of Sara's request, the nurse says,

"Hang in there a minute. I'll be right back." She returns with a huge maternity sanitary napkin. "This is what we use on our older incontinent kids."

"The old elephant pads. I remember them well. I sure won't tell Sara what this is. Thanks a lot, Marshall."

Suzanne waits outside while we ready Sara for the ride. Red-robed, reclining, forty cents in hand, she's off. I push the cart, Suzanne handles the pump.

We park outside the cafeteria; our rig won't negotiate the doorway. "Give me the money, Sissy. I'll buy the pop."

"I'll buy it myself," she says. "Help me up, Mama."

Long, gaunt, hunched, Sara scurries into the lunchroom, using the IV pole for support. She snatches the pop, plunks down her money and scuttles back to her cart. "Get me back fast, Mama. I have to go again."

"Let go if you have to, Sissy."

"Faster," she begs. "Just move faster."

When we leave the elevator I take the pump from Suzanne, who's having trouble with our fast pace. "Meet you at the room, sweetie," I promise. And Sara and I fly home.

Laid out, breathless, but proud of her pop, Sara says, "Suzanne, let's play paper dolls."

Mostly Suzanne plays while Sara watches. I tell Marshall about the expedition. "She walked in by herself?" Marshall exclaims.

"She did," I boast. "And now she's actually playing with Suzanne."

"A red-letter day," Marshall says. "The docs will be pleased to hear about this."

Sara naps when Suzanne leaves. "I kind of don't mind my king-size diapers," she drowses. "Order up some more."

At nine Sara asks for another bath. "The warm water feels so good." Eagerly I prepare for it, because I love the cozy conversation in that steamy tub room. Sara lies on the banana cart and I haul the heavy pole to our hideaway. My Biafran baby girl stretches out in the bathtub, bony, swollen-bellied and beautiful. She groans at the soft knock on the door.

"Who is it?" I call.

"Susan."

"Oh, let her in," Sara urges.

I unlock and admonish, "Why aren't you home with your husband?"

"He's working late, and I knew you'd like a cup of tea." She hands me a paper cup of minty brew, and settles onto the floor. Sara smiles and asks Susan why she didn't bring a third cup of tea.

"Oh, never mind," Sara says. "I'll just lie here and think about what I'm going to eat when I get out of here."

"Tell us about it, Sara," Susan says.

"A corndog on the ferry boat, A&W root beer, spaghetti, Three Crabs fish and chips, yogurt and Reese's Peanut Butter Cups."

"Gag," I gasp.

Dr. Marshall claps, "Wonderful!"

Our party is festive. We admire Sara's beautiful new skin, and she basks, like a fish in a pond, under the warmth of our praises. Susan bends to pet Sara's shiny head goodnight. I follow her outside the door, and we squeeze tight. "I know the worst is over," she says. "I really believe it."

"Get me out of here," Sara demands. "My new skin is prune skin."

"Coming, your majesty," I warble. And Susan Marshall and I hug one last time. We laugh big happy tears.

But Wednesday Sara suffers. The diarrhea turns more urgent, more explosive, and we resort to using a bedpan. "Maybe we overdid it yesterday, Sissy," I comfort. But my insides are grabbing again. And I am so afraid.

The doctors are solemn outside our door, studying Sara's charts. They don't come in this morning so I seek them out. I snag Ralph as the group moves on to Big Joe's room. "What do they think, Ralph? I feel very scared."

"We're doing all we can, Carol. Her output is incredible, and that's the real concern. If only we could get a handle on that, everyone would feel better. I wish I could tell you everything's going to be OK. But I just don't know."

I feel those old cold shivers coming on again when Dr. Johnson catches my elbow and says, "I'd like to talk to you and Sara, Carol."

Sara smiles at her beloved physician as he faces up close to her. "How are you, sweetheart? Kinda worn out today? Well, that's OK, darlin'. Just rest up. Sara, I'm gonna be gone for a week. I'm going to visit Saint Jude's Children's Hospital in Memphis, Tennessee."

Sara looks worried, her eyes fill and she moves her head back and forth on her pillow. "No," she whispers.

"I have instructions for you, Sara," Dr. J. says softly. "I want you to rest, watch a little TV and keep your nurses in line while I'm gone. Take good care of your mommy and I'll be back before you know it."

"I want you to stay," Sara weeps.

"And I would if I could, darlin'. Dr. Nugent will keep special watch over you and I'll call Clinic for a report every day. Surprise me, Sara, and be ready to sip a few c.c.'s when I get back."

"OK," she says. "Hurry home."

When I call Walt this evening from the pay phone, so Sara can't hear, I am beyond help. "Things are falling apart around here," I bawl.

"Get a hold of yourself," Walt says. "Talk to me."

I tell him Dr. J. is leaving, I can't sleep, and the night nurses are new and inexperienced. "I have to stay awake to protect Sara," I sob. "And she's bad, Walt, real bad."

"Carol, that just can't be. You were so excited last night. You said she'd turned the corner."

"Well, I was wrong," I wail.

"Honey, maybe you're just seeing things tough because you're so tired. Let the nurses help you with Sara tonight."

"Didn't you hear me?" I snap. "They don't know what they're doing. I have to guard Sara."

"Carol, I'm worried about you. You can't help Sara if you don't get a grip on yourself. I'll come over right now."

"No, no." I pull myself together. "We're OK."

When I hang up, I lay my head on the little phone desk and cry some more. Familiar long thin hands massage my shoulders. Sue and little Carrie are here on their evening visit. "Come on," Sue says. "Tell me all about it."

After a bit, we head upstairs for our nightly chitchat outside 315. I hear a faint, "Mama," and bolt up to be with my daughter. "Carrie's root beer," Sara directs. "Order up her root beer.''

Every night when Carrie drops by, Sara offers up root beer. In remembrance of their dancing days.

Sue loves me goodnight. She'll call in the morning as usual. ''Be brave, old friend,'' she says.

And I choke, ''I'll try.''

Just before my shower, Dr. Hoshi tiptoes next to Sara's bed. ''I made for you, Sala,'' he whispers, then pulls a pile of origami cranes from his pocket. ''In Japan, crane mean good luck.''

''Thank you,'' Sara says. ''You must've folded all day.''

''On this one, maybe,'' he laughs and holds forth a tiny, perfectly creased purple kangaroo. ''His name Dr. J. and he watch over you until Len Johnson come back from St. Jude's. Rest now, Sala.''

But there's no sleep tonight. Sara is restless and in pain when she urinates. Night shift is short-staffed and Sara fills the potty pans faster than they can be tested and emptied.

''It's bad enough she has to go so often, but it's sickening to have to use a dirty pot. Teach me to run the tests and I'll handle it myself.''

''I'm so sorry,'' the poor nurse worries. ''It's just that we don't have enough people working tonight. I'll be right in.''

Some time in the night I wake to watch the frazzled new nurse inject the Prednisone into Sara's line.

''Prep it,'' I hiss. ''You didn't prep the connection. You're supposed to leave a wipe on for two minutes before you open the line.''

''I'm sorry,'' she sweats. ''I forgot. I'm running late on meds and I just forgot.''

Thursday morning I grab Ralph and tattle on the night-shift nurse. "I don't mean to get her in trouble, Ralph, because it's not really her fault. They're so short-handed at night. There's gonna be a big mistake made, and I don't want it to be with my kid."

"You're right to tell someone, Carol. I'll pass it along."

Sara needs a platelet transfusion this morning. Another big blow. Up until now her blood counts have been steady—a positive sign, according to Dr. Johnson.

"I want Daddy," Sara whispers.

"He's coming tomorrow, Sissy. Right after school."

"Call him now," she insists.

"He's not home, honey. I'll talk to him tonight."

"Tell him to hurry," she murmurs. "He needs to be here."

Jeannette has trouble hearing Sara's blood pressure today. When I look frantic, Jeannette smiles, "I think maybe I'm a little deaf. Sometimes I have this trouble." And she calls in Nurse Marshall.

"Let's get an infant cuff," Marshall suggests. "These arms are pretty scrawny."

"There it is," Jeannette sighs. "Good girl, Sara."

Marshall sits by Sara, holding her hand.

"It's very sad, Marshall."

"Yes, it is, Sara. Very sad." Marshall nods.

I have a bad pain in my chest and I wonder if hearts really break. I get up fast and leave the room. I wander the third floor a while, looking for a place to be alone. And wind up in the chapel.

And I pray. I pray hard. I pray for something I've never prayed for before. "God," I pray, "I want her to live and be well. And if that can happen I will wait forever. But if it can't happen, don't make her suffer any more."

I pray for resolution. I pray for peace.

Outside the padded double doors of the chapel I find Bob McLaughlin, the COH chaplain. "Come with me, Carol," he says. "Let's talk."

In the little conference room where it all began I confess the wretched little prayer I prayed. "I really didn't mean it, you know. I don't want her anything but well. It's just that I'm so tired and she's so sad."

Chaplain McLaughlin nods and says my prayer was a good prayer. "I've sensed a little of the same feeling in Sara this past week. I have no magic words, Carol, but I'm reminded of the father of another little cancer kid I knew. He came to me one day for a scripture reference. 'The same damn Bible verse keeps running through my head,' he told me—

> They shall mount up with wings like eagles,
> They shall run and not be weary . . .

Then he looked at me and asked, 'What's with the eagles and the running, Chaplain? We're at the end of the line, you know.'

"I finished the verse for him . . .

> They shall walk and not faint.

Maybe that's where you and Sara are, Carol. Not flying, not running. But not fainting, either. Still in the race."

We sit silent for a few minutes and then I say, "Thank you very much. I'd better get back to Sara." And he says he'll look in on us in the morning.

Sara is just as I left her, lying on her right side, snuggled under her quilt. Very still. "I have to go again, Mama."

"All right, sweetheart." I smile, unplugging the pumps and starting to lift her.

"Oh, Mama," she worries. "I'm so dizzy. I think I'm going to faint."

"We'll use the bedpan this time, Sissy."

When we finish she asks, "Where'd you go when you left me? I worried."

"I was visiting the chaplain," I begin. And then I crack like a shattered mirror. Screaming out in all directions. "I'm so sorry, Sara. I don't want you to hurt any more. I'm so sorry we did this to you. I'm so sorry. I can't help you. Forgive me, Sara. I love you. . . ." I blubber.

"You're talking nonsense. Get control of yourself," she orders.

"I can't," I sob.

"Then get out of here until you can."

"OK," I bawl and hustle out the door.

Nurse Marshall sits with Sara while I pull it together. And when I return, they both smile. "You need a nap, old girl," Sara says. "No Johnny Carson for you tonight."

"Right," I laugh.

Tonight Sara suffers from diarrhea, painful urination, low blood pressure and unquenchable thirst. The H.A. line malfunctions; blood won't draw. And two days of mail lie unopened.

"Call Daddy," she whispers over and over again. "He needs to be here."

Shortly before Walt's Friday afternoon arrival, a resident dentist and a couple of intern groupies burst in for a routine mouth exam.

Following previous checkups, Sara and I have chuckled over the dentists' oral fixation. "If they ever drew a picture of me, Mama," Sara laughs, "it would be just a big set of no-cavity chompers and a few 'sliightly receded' gums!"

But today they are more than dullards we can mock later. The leader of the pack pries, prods, then preaches his findings. "Excellent," he hisses through his own pearly whites, "just excellent. She's been faithful with her mouth care and I detect no oral ulcers. Have a look-see," he invites his fellow flunkies.

Ashamed to have allowed the first attack, but better late than never, I crouch on my bed and mutter, "Please don't touch her again." They step back, in case I spring, but still don't see the big picture.

"Looks great, just great. Keep up the good work," they chant, sliding out the door.

"I promise I'll never marry a dentist," Sara murmurs. And rests again.

Marshall peeks in and reports, "A tall dark handsome stranger is headed your way."

"Hi, Daddy," Sara exhales.

"Hi, Beaners." Walt studies her and I study Walt: sallow-skinned, ancient-eyed, punched down like bread dough. He takes her in. "It's OK now," he whispers. "Dad's here."

And she sleeps.

We buy sandwiches from the machines tonight and pick them apart outside Sara's door. Little David Ayers peek-a-boos from his isolation room across the hall, but Walt's eyes are on Sara.

"Daddy," she calls softly, and he cannonballs to her bed-side.

"I'm right here, Sissy."

"Daddy, I want you to care for me tonight. So Mama can sleep."

"There's nothing I'd rather do, Beans."

Catnip Karen is on tonight. "You're lucky," I tell Walt. "She's the only one who empties the pot as fast as we fill it."

Walt bolts at Sara's every murmur. I hawk-eye his technique to make sure he's doing everything the right way, my way. But I relax a little when I hear Sara say, "I like how you carry me, Dad."

Around two, Walt calls for help. Sara has fainted on the toilet. I squeeze in to wipe her bottom while Walt kneels in front of her, supporting his groaning, spent little daughter.

We stumble her back into bed. "It hurts real bad to pee, Mama. And I gotta pee all the time."

"I'll get help, sweetheart. Promise."

Storming into the hall, I attack Paula, our night nurse. "Darn it, Paula. This is the third night in a row it's hurt her to pee and nobody does anything about it. If she's got a urinary infection why don't they treat it?"

"I've notified the intern on call," she stews. "I'll call him again. Be right back."

Walt helps Sara onto the bedpan while I spy on Paula phoning the intern. "Oh, no," Sissy moans. "I'm fainting again." Then, "I hurt. I hurt." And a few drops tinkle into the stainless steel.

"Make them do something out there," I beg Walt. And he heads for the nurses' station.

"Sissy, honey, how 'bout if we put one of those special diapers on you. Then we won't have to worry about getting you on a bedpan." I suggest.

She nods consent, so I wash and diaper her, then sit in the

plastic chair by her bedside.

Walt says that Paula says that the intern says that since there's no temp, he doubts it's infection. Most likely a delayed reaction to the Cytoxan.

"I don't care what it's caused from," I fume, "I want something done about her pain. A sedative. A catheter. Something."

"Paula says she'll make sure the doctors are informed of this whole mess first thing in the morning," Walt sighs.

Sara seems peaceful, so we climb back into bed for a minute's rest. But when we come awake, it's grey dawn of Saturday, September 20, and Catnip Karen's taking vital signs. "Karen!" I gasp. "She hasn't had diarrhea since two this morning! That's the longest she's held in weeks."

"Great," says Karen. "But Carol, she started running fever at four this morning, and her blood pressure's way down. The doc's on his way."

I sit beside Sara while Walt dresses in the bathroom. "Oh, Mama," she wails, forsaken, "I'm going to die."

"No-no-no, Sara," I reprimand, like when she was two and touching my Hummel. "It's just another hard time, like so many times before. And we always come through, Sissy. We're tough."

And then, not frightened, not sad. Just matter of fact. "No, Mama. I'm dying. I'm really dying."

"Shhh, silly girl," I say. And she offers a small pitying smile. Then closes her eyes.

Karen fusses around Sara while Walt shaves and I dress. "My hair's a mess. Think I'll shampoo," I announce, and jerk on the faucet.

"It's hard to concentrate with that noise," Sara whispers.

I say, "Sure, honey. I'll use the public rest room."

I say, "Be right back." Like maybe we're back home and I'm off for a loaf of bread.

When I return, the intern is wringing his hands and Sara's puking into a pan. I plant myself beside her and take in her flushed plumped-out cheeks and wise brown eyes. Her breathing is rapid and shallow. Labored, I think. This is what they call labored breathing.

Some time passes and when I look up, Dan Niebrugge is talking to Walt, and Diane Nugent stands at the head of Sara's bed. Which is really the foot of Sara's bed, I think, since it's been turned around since "Little House" night.

"Hey, Sara," Diane says. "We're gonna need some X rays. And we'll get a little oxygen for you so you can breathe easier."

"Is it pneumonia?" I whisper, wiping Sara's lips with a wet washcloth.

"That's a possibility," Diane answers.

"But her color's good. Isn't it?" I plead, touching Sara's rosy cheek.

"I'd like that blood back where it belongs," the doctor says. "We're going to administer a drug called Dopamine to try to get the pressure up."

X ray sets up while Walt and I hover alone over Sara. The doctors huddle at the nurses' station. Dr. Chard, the head hematologist, has joined them.

I strip Sara for the X rays, don a lead apron, and shift her into position after position as the technician clicks his machine. On-off, on-off, on-off.

Respiratory Therapy arrives next and sets up oxygen for Sara. Dr. Nugent holds the tube to Sara's nose while I hold the emesis pan to her mouth and continue wiping her lips. Walt hangs near the clump of attending physicians, waiting for The Cure.

There's a huge plate of doughnuts on the side table and Nurse Marshall is on the other side of Sara's bed, wearing jeans and a blouse.

"How did you know?" I ask.

"I didn't," she says. "I had to bring Bill in this morning and thought you'd like the doughnuts. I didn't know. But I'm glad I'm here."

Bill, Marshall's intern husband, joins the knot of people outside our door.

Suddenly Sara coughs, chokes and bright red blood fills the emesis pan. Sara's eyes snap, surprised. My eyes search out Diane Nugent and she says, "We'll need some platelets. Fast." Marshall hustles out to order them.

Sara hiccups little blots of blood and I dab the corner of her mouth.

Hiccup-dab, hiccup-dab, hiccup-dab.

"We're going to need another line in Sara," Dr. Nugent says. "And I think we'll head up to Intensive Care to insert it."

"Why another line?" I ask.

"Antibiotics," she answers. "We didn't see any pneumonia, and that's good, but something's cooking and we've got to try to treat it. We need another entry . . ."

"When?" I interrupt.

"Soon," she nods.

Hiccup-dab, hiccup-dab, hiccup-dab.

"Mama, I'm scared."

"Of what, Sissy? Intensive Care? What will happen there?"

She just looks into my eyes.

"Oh, Sissy," I say, petting her hand. "I'll stay with you, always. And remember what we believe. No matter what, you're safe."

"I know that, Mama." And she smiles. Such a beautiful trusting little smile. "But Dr. Marshall will be so disappointed." She smiles a sad smile and closes her eyes.

Walt comes to hold the oxygen while Dr. Nugent joins the confab in the hall.

Hiccup-dab, hiccup-dab, hiccup-dab.

"I feel good," Sara says, surprised.

Hiccup-dab, hiccup-dab, hiccup-dab.

"Oh, I'm feeling fine now."

Finally, Diane says, "ICU is ready."

And Sara says, "Is it time to go now? I'm ready to go. I want my pillow and my quilt." Like she's headed off to camp.

"How about we take the whole bed?" Dr. Nugent swings the head of the bed around (but it's really the foot of the bed) and leads the parade. Walt with the oxygen, I with the emesis bowl.

Hiccup-dab, hiccup-dab, hiccup-dab.

The view from ICU is incredible.

"Oh, Sara," I gasp. "It's the best room in the house. Can you see, sweetheart?"

"Yes," she says. "But the light's too bright. Please close the curtain. Too bright."

I fiddle with the curtains while new nurses hook Sara to new machines. Walt stands on one side of the bed, Dr. Nugent on the other with a stethoscope pressed to Sara's back. An anesthesiologist prepares to insert an arterial line through Sara's hand.

Sara opens her eyes and locks in on Walt. "Don't worry, Dad," she says. "I'm safe now."

"Can't I worry just a little bit?" Walt asks.

"No," she whispers, firm. "Not even a little bit."

And she closes her eyes.

Dr. Chard calls Walt to the doorway and I take Walt's place beside Sara while the anesthesiologist preps her hand. "Step back just a bit," he says, and I move to the right as he makes the incision in Sara's slender-fingered piano-hand.

Horrible buzzers whine as I lurch toward Walt, and people blur by, shoving me out the door. I look back as Sara's body, naked except for rosebud underpants, jolts off the bed.

"Code," somebody says, and Dr. Chard grabs my arm as I try to reach back for Sara. When I fall on my knees Dr. Chard and Walt lift me up by the armpits and carry me, like a naughty child, into a conference room.

"I promised I'd stay with her," I bawl. "Let me go."

"She doesn't know," Ron Chard promises. "They need room to work."

"Don't let them hurt her any more," I beg. "Leave her alone."

"It may not be over, Carol," the kind-faced, grey haired doctor says. "Let them try."

The three of us sit in silence, our hands heaped together on the table. And after a while a nurse comes in and we get up to meet her at the door. "We have her hooked up to life-support, but there's no brain activity . . ."

"Let her go. Just let her go," I say. And Walt nods.

Walt leaves then. Bears the news home to B-3. Ron Chard and I sit alone. "I feel funny," I say. And he nods. "Like a tremendous weight is gone from me. And that if I stand up, my feet might leave the ground. Oh Sara, I'm so sorry I feel this way!"

"It's OK," our doctor says. "The weight is gone from Sara, too. It's OK."

"Right," I nod. "She's free from it. She's safe."

We sit a while.

"Do you want an autopsy performed?" Dr. Chard says.

"Would you learn anything that might help some other kid?" I ask.

"No," he answers softly. "We're pretty certain she died of an intestinal perforation. There's really nothing to be gained."

"Then no, just leave her be."

We sit a while.

"I know it's cold where they're taking her. She hates to be cold," I worry. "But that's silly. She's not really in there any more, is she?"

"No," agrees Dr. Chard.

Nancy comes in and we hug, long hard hugs. "I'm going to see her," Nancy says. "Do you want to come with me?"

"No," I answer. "But will you bring me her quilt?"

Nancy comes back in a few minutes, red-eyed but stiff-lipped, and hands me Sara's carefully bundled quilt. And Sara's gold chain. With the heart that matches mine.

SIX

W E packed up Sara's hospital room one last time. Nancy came in and told us to go home. "I want to finish up here," she whispered.

·

At the ferry dock, we used a pay phone to have the Verstegens paged at the U.W. football game. "Don't come by the hospital," we said. "We're not there. Sara died," we said.

·

On the ferryboat, Walt shook his head. "I bet the news will somehow beat us home."

·

When we pulled into the folks' driveway, the minister's car was there. "Told you so," Walt said.

Andy looked up from his Legos. "Mama, you're home! But where's Sissy?" They were statue-still at the dining-room table. I sat in the maple rocker and took Andy on my lap.

"Sara died, Andy."

And he jerked from my embrace and said, "You promised she wouldn't die!"

And I answered, "Not true, Andy."

"Well, you said you didn't think she'd die," he whimper-ed. Then buried his head in my birthday sweater and cried mad, sad little-boy tears.

•

On the way home from Grandma and Grandpa's house, Andy said, "What will we do with all Sara's toys?"

And I asked, "What do you think we should do with them, Andy?"

"We could move them to my room," he grinned.

•

He chose Sara's blanket and her old brown bear. And he slept with them that night.

•

The Verstegens stopped in on their way home from Seattle. They brought me a new blue nightgown. And I wore it to bed that night.

•

Sunday morning we cried. Andy snuggled into our bed, patted my new blue nightgown and said, "It's not time to cry now, Mama. Be happy. Sara doesn't hurt any more."

Monday morning Walt went to school. I washed, dried and ironed Sara's "Little House" dress and bonnet. And the yellow quilt, too. Then I put them in a grocery bag.

•

Monday morning I walked Andy to kindergarten. He carried a show and share. I carried the grocery bag. The sun shone and I felt good.

•

Monday morning little children hugged my knees and said, "I'm so sorry about Sara."

Teachers hugged my shoulders and said, "It's good to see you. I'm glad you're here." The sun shone and I felt good.

•

Monday morning Rita walked with me to the funeral chapel. She carried a purse. I carried the grocery bag. She left with her purse. But I went home empty-handed.

•

Monday afternoon *The Daily News* called. I sat on the kitchen floor and detailed Sara's death and dying to a stranger who didn't talk back. And when we hung up, the sun shone and I felt good.

•

Monday night I lay alone on our bed with the lights out. Walt was in the family room with school work. I watched "Little House on the Prairie." I watched Laura marry Almanzo. It was dark and I felt bad.

Tuesday Elmer came over and we planned Sara's Thursday memorial service. "We want it for children, Elmer. Not sad. It mustn't be sad."

•

Wednesday Dr. Johnson called. "I am devastated," he said. "We need to get together. You have questions that need answers."

•

"No, no," I said. "What good are questions now? She's all gone. Questions won't bring her back."

"I'll call in a few weeks and we'll set a meeting date," he said. "Please know I'm just so sorry . . ."

•

Thursday Walt stayed home from school. Our families gathered. Dressed in Sunday best. We lunched at Grandma's house. Ate food our friends prepared.

•

Sue and little Carrie, Nurse Nancy and rec-room Patty arrived from Seattle. They were family that day.

•

The church overflowed with roses. With children. The high-school choir sang strong. Sara's kindergarten teacher soloed. Put Kenny to shame. "Love Lifted Me" never had it so good. We all sang "The Magic Penny" and "Morning Has Broken."

The little children came up front and settled on the rug. "I've thought of some worries you might have," began Elmer. "Some questions. Well, maybe I have some answers. How about this one. Did Sara know she was dying? Or did death just sneak up and grab her away? She knew. And you know how I know she knew?"

The little children shook their heads.

"Because Sara said so. 'I'm dying, Mama.' That's what she said.

"Question number two. Did it hurt for Sara to die? To be sure, Sara hurt while she was sick. But did it hurt for Sara to die? Nope. And you know how I know?"

The little children shook their heads.

"Because Sara said so. 'I feel fine now. Oh, I'm feeling fine.' That's what she said.

"Here's question number three. Was Sara afraid to die? Well, she wasn't. And you know how I know?"

The little children shouted, smiling, "Because Sara said so!"

And we all nodded and smiled too.

"Right," grinned Elmer. "She said, 'Don't worry, Dad. I'm safe now.' No. Sara wasn't afraid."

•

We stood outside the church. "We love you," they said. The sun shone and we felt good.

•

Every day I called B-3 to ask after Big Joe. One morning Karen said, "He's much better today. He died this morning."

In October Taki and Jennifer relapsed.

•

My boys filled their days with school. My days condemned to "hope this helps" books, sympathy cards, old photographs.

•

My boys filled their nights with TV and Legos. My nights consumed by frantic phone calls to the "listening ladies." They heard my story over and over again. While their friendship divided up my grief.

•

Sara's bedroom. Done-in a day. Artwork boxed, drawers emptied, closets stripped. But the dolls stayed. With the little red velvet coat. And the sweet smell of Sara.

•

We dressed carefully for dinner at Verstegens. Our first evening out. We ate carefully, drank carefully, laughed carefully. Sturdy little robots. We cried all the way home.

•

Every day I visited the cemetary. To sit on Sara's ground.

•

When they finally placed the marker on her grave, I took Andy up to see it.

SARA BETH KRUCKEBERG
1971–1980
BELOVED DAUGHTER AND SISTER

Why'd you write just that?'' he asked.

"What do you mean, 'just that'?" I asked back.

"Well, she was a lot more things, ya know. Beloved daughter, sister, granddaughter, niece, cousin and friend. A lot more things, ya know."

•

In November, we journeyed back to COH. Restless. Filled with questions. As Dr. Johnson knew we would be. We met for an hour with our physician and friend. Talked good times and bad. "Children have died and will continue to die, Carol," he said. "But Sara did it her way. Have you ever considered writing it all down?"

•

Nurse Marshall came for lunch. "Oh, Marshall. Do I take her photographs off the wall or do I put more up? Do I box her artwork or do I frame it? What's right and what's wrong?"

"Do what feels right for you now, Carol. Some day if it's no good any more, you'll know. And you'll fix it. Trust your instincts," she said.

•

We asked to donate a mural to COH. In memory of Sara. We chose a Jessie Wilcox Smith painting of a brown-haired little girl watching fairies in a pond.

"Why that one?" asked the hospital artist.

"Sara saw fairies in ponds," we smiled.

•

One sad Sunday I dug out Sara's incomplete third-grade poetry collection, stored in a wooden recipe box. There, on a three-by-five index card, was Sara's hastily scrawled note of apology to her teacher. "Did not finish. Correct on what I did."

On the phone one day I told Sandy, "I wish the grass would grow on Sara's grave." The brown-dirt gash made the hurt so fresh. The next day Sandy's husband laid turf on Sara's ground.

•

Nighttime. Back-to-back parenthesis, we cried separate tears.

"I'm sorry," Walt wept. "I'm so sorry."

"It's not your fault," I sobbed.

"But I'm just so sorry."

Shut up, don't say that again, I wanted to scream. But I didn't.

•

Dinnertime. Reaching across her empty chair to join hands for prayer. Night after night.

•

During dessert Andy announced, "I don't want to be 'one' forever."

And Walt and I nodded.

"We'll get on that, Big Boy," I promised.

•

In bed Walt whispered, "Is it time to call an adoption agency? Will people think it's too soon?

"Well, the hell with them," Walt said. "I don't want to be 'one' forever, either."

The Western Association of Concerned Adoptive Parents sent the requested forms by return mail.

•

One month after Sara died I woke to the alarm clock ringing. "I slept all night!"

"Good. That's very good," Walt said.

"No, no. Maybe I'm forgetting her. And I can't let that happen."

•

One day Matt and Andy lay bored in the bedroom. "Guess we can't have our lemonade stand any more," Matt sighed. And Andy nodded. "Since Sara was the only one who knew how to make change."

•

Andy suffered night wakings. Often we found him wrapped in his kitty blanket, rocking, tuned to old horror movies, test patterns or pre-dawn religion.

•

Over Cheerios I said, "Andy, you mustn't get up at night any more."

"I have to, Mom," he answered.

"No. You must just lie there until you go back to sleep."

Then he cried. "But Mama, in the day, when I think of Sissy I can be busy and get rid of her. But at night, when I think of Sissy there's nothing else to do. She just stays in my mind."

Just before Halloween, Mrs. McDaniel came by with nut bread. "Too bad I forgot the nuts," she laughed.

"The grapevine has it, Carol, that the piano bothers you some."

"I miss the sound of Sara practicing more than anything," I confessed. "I can hardly look at that piano."

"I think I can help you over it," she said. "I'd like to offer you a scholarship. My eyes aren't what they used to be and I need some help. If you will play the second piano parts for recitals, I will give you lessons. Call and let me know if we have a deal."

•

At dinner Walt said, "Old fox! She needs your help like Librace needs candles."

Andy asked, "May I take lessons, too?"

In November the piano got a workout.

•

One morning Andy named the baby. "I want to name her my favorite girl's name," he chattered.

"Let's have it," I replied, loading plates into the dishwasher.

"Sara," he said. "We'll call her Sara."

I sat at the table beside him. "It's a beautiful name, Big Boy. But we'll have to choose another. A brand-new person needs a brand-new name."

"Molly," he said. "After one of my old girlfriends."

"Love it," I laughed. "Molly Rose. We'll check with Dad."

In November Defawn dropped by. "The flower shop's getting busy," she said. "I need some extra help through Christmas. Would it be possible, Carol, for you to come in?"

•

At dinner Walt said, "Old fox! She needs you like Pasadena needs roses."

Andy asked, "May I work, too?"

•

In December Andy made a wreath for Sara's grave.

"He must've used twenty bucks' worth of Christmas decorations, Fawnie," I worried.

"No matter," she answered. "It's perfect, Andy. Sara would've loved it."

And he grinned proud.

•

It looked, sounded and smelled like Christmas. The flower shop was Wonderland. I worked a little and laughed a lot. At 5:30 I went home.

•

At kindergarten conference Mrs. Kathleen said, "Aggressive tendencies. Pushy on the playground. Can't seem to reach him."

•

Another fight today. "Oh, Andy," I scolded. "You have to get along with your friends."

"I don't want to get along with nobody," he cried. "I only want to get along with Sissy."

•

Mrs. Kathleen said, "Andy was quiet when we discussed Christmas plans."

"Maybe he thinks we're not celebrating this year," I said. "I guess we'd better decorate."

•

Our tree was a shaggy Douglas fir. Grim-faced, we hung her handmade ornaments. The cotton-bearded Santa face, sequined little candy cane, glittered plaster of Paris pretzel. And the angel. Joyous wings, little bare feet, and a lopsided halo.

•

At the bottom of the Christmas box was a faded homemade Christmas card. "To Mom and Dad. Good luck this year. Love, Sara."

•

"I want to go to bed and wake up when Christmas is over," I told Defawn.

"I'll bet you do," she said.

Not "Cheer up, Bucko. You'll get by."

Not "Next year will be better."

Not "Be strong for Walt and Andy."

"I'll bet you do," she said.

•

Andy asked, "Will Sara get presents this year?"

And I answered, "No."

"Not even just one?" he said.

And I answered, "No."

•

At church they sang, "O Little Town of Bethlehem." Sara's favorite carol. And the Sacred Dancers danced. Sara's good friends. I ran away to the rest room.

•

Pressed against a toilet stall, Elmer's wife held me like a baby. I cried mascara onto her white dress. She cried too.

•

We skipped church until January.

•

Christmas day. Two red stockings, one white. The pink one put away on a top shelf. While Andy and Walt ran race cars, I burrowed into Sara's room. Cradled her dolls, pawed through her artwork. Sniffed out the scent of her.

•

The family gathered for traditions. Grandma's crab dip, home-sewn and -grown gifts, let-the-youngest-open-first, and "Heart and Soul" on the piano one too many times.

•

The cousins posed for Uncle Walt's annual Christmas snapshot. And this year there was more room on the couch.

The end of December Marge called. Jennifer's Christmas in Disneyland was marred by blood transfusions. Marge said, "She looks sick."

•

New Year's Day Marge called. Jennifer's back in COH. Marge said, "She looks sicker."

•

Jennifer called the abdominal tumor "my pet rock." She said she could feel it growing. She smiled woozy from the morphine.

•

On January 7 Nurse Marshall called and said, "Jennifer just died. Marge wanted you to know."

•

That morning a friend came by for coffee. "How about a rain check. Just leaving," I lied. Then I locked the door, pulled the curtains, played sad songs and cried.

I cried all day long. Not for Jennifer and Sara. For Marge and me.

•

"We can't use our Kauai condo this year," my best friend from Bellingham said. "We want you to have it for two weeks. Just let me know when, and I'll make the reservations."

•

That evening Walt said, "No way. We can't afford the air fare." Then he figured our income tax.

"Our tax refund equals the air fare, almost to the penny," Walt said. "I don't believe in 'meant to be's,' but maybe the Old Boy's trying to tell us something."

•

"June 12 to 24. You're all booked," said my best friend from Bellingham. "Send me a postcard."

•

Winter quarter writing class started Wednesday night. I took a new pen, yellow legal pad and a nervous stomach.

•

Late Wednesday night Walt whispered, "Can't sleep? Thinking of Sissy?"

"Thinking of writing about Sissy," I said. "And it feels good."

"Better get it done before the baby comes," Walt warned. And we laughed.

•

In February our adoption home-study was completed and we awaited word of a promised biracial baby girl.

•

One piano-lesson Tuesday Mrs. McDaniel greeted me in a brand-new curly wig. "Should've taken Sara's word for it. Wigs are hot, itchy and don't look like your real hair, anyway!" Mrs. McD. smiled.

"Wednesday night's the highlight of your week, isn't it?" Walt asked as I stapled my copies for writing class.

"Maybe so. Do you mind?"

"I'm happy for you," Walt sighed.

•

In the spring Walt taught hard. Walt taught well. And when he talked, he talked to his school kids.

•

I stripped the pink rosebud wallpaper off Sara's bedroom walls, and rolled on green floral. Walt moved in the crib and I plopped Sara's favorite doll, Big Annie, into it.

"No, Mom," Andy said. "A brand-new person needs a brand-new doll."

•

Andy chose tan fabric for the face and black yarn for the hair. "Let's call it Big Brown Annie," he giggled.

•

The baby's room just needed the baby.

•

We went to the Jacobses' for Jana's birthday dinner. Andy played all evening with Jill. Listening to them killed me. I couldn't look at Walt.

On the way home Andy drowsed in the back seat. "I loved tonight," he said. "It was almost like having Sissy back."

Regularly I called the agency for news of our biracial baby girl.

"Have patience," they laughed.

•

One May morning at Mom's I dug through my wallet for Andy's new school picture. A tiny sealed Little Kitty envelope fell into my lap. I snatched it up and opened it.

Dear Mom and Dad,
I love you and
I love Andy too!
Well bye,
Love,
Sara

•

All the way home I cried. I love you too, Sara. Now let me go.

•

Mom promised to flower Sara's grave while we were on vacation. Still, it was hard to go.

•

Our first week on Kauai Andy talked often of Sara.

"Sissy'd be scared of these waves."

"Sissy'd love those hula skirts."

"Remember how Sissy said 'coconot' instead of 'coconut'?"

He had a nightmare in the middle of the week, sobbed, "I wish Sissy was sleeping in that other bed."

The second week on Kauai Andy studied Hawaiian babies. "Do you think she'll look like that one? Or that one? Or that one?" he said.

•

Walt bought Hawaiian print fabric so I could make Molly Rose a quilt.

•

I sat in the shallow ocean with the little grains of sand.

•

On August 7, Sara's tenth birthday, we put roses on the church altar, sent roses to B-3 in remembrance of "my best birthday ever," plucked roses from the bushes in our yard.

•

On August 7, Sara's tenth birthday, I lay in the sun and thought how much easier the day would be if my Molly Rose were here.

•

A week later the phone rang. Biracial baby girl, born August 6. "Are you interested?"

•

August 15 Molly Rose came home. Andy fashioned her birth announcement. A curly-headed baby surrounded by hearts.

Captioned, "Love Never Ends."

Today I sit and think of Sara. Still lonely. Still sad. Still wishing her into my life again. And I work to do what she did so well. To choose where there is choice. Laughter, life, love. To keep the game going. To trust.

•

"Did not finish. Correct on what I did."

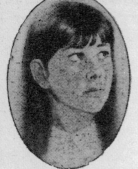

Become a winner at love, work, and play.

Dr. Irene C. Kassorla

A distinguished, practicing psychologist, Dr. Kassorla describes the differences between winning and losing personalities. She first pinpoints the skills and attitudes that carry winners to the top, and then illustrates how *everyone* can develop such skills and use them successfully in love, work, and play. Dr. Kassorla also includes enlightening, instructive interviews with winners from many fields: Malcolm Forbes, Diane von Furstenberg, Jack Lemmon, Bruce Jenner, Bob Woodward, and many more.

You won't be the same after *you* go for it!

12752-1-30 $3.95

"Deeply moving and beautifully written. A triumph of life over death!"
—*Marya Mannes*

ERIC

by Doris Lund

The true story of a seventeen-year-old boy's courageous struggle against leukemia, as told by his mother. "Eric was the kind of . . . kid who could accept a doctor's shattering diagnosis yet go on to attend college, play varsity athletics, take a cross-country trip and fall in love . . . Eric's drawings, included in the book, make his story even more poignant. His mother describes his four-year struggle with unflinching honesty."—*Publishers Weekly*

94586-9-46 $2.95

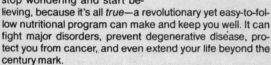